"if you dominate the bve
what happens"

Successful German Soccer Tactics

1. have you worked hard to get the ball back quickly?

2. have you made consistently good decisions?

3. did you outplay your opponent both w/ & w/out the ball?

a) possess a relentless workrate
b) consistently striving to be the best
c) be open minded
d) be humble

For my father, who now watches the most beautiful game
in the world from way up high.

Timo Jankowski

SUCCESSFUL GERMAN
SOCCER TACTICS

The Best Match Plans for a Winning Team

Meyer & Meyer Sport

Original title: Matchplan Fußball
Translation: AAA Translation, St. Louis

British Library Cataloguing in Publication Data
A catalogue record for this book is available from the British Library

Successful German Soccer Tactics
Maidenhead: Meyer & Meyer Sport (UK) Ltd., 2015
ISBN: 978-1-78255-062-4

© 2015 by Meyer & Meyer Sports (UK) Ltd.
Aachen, Auckland, Beirut, Cairo, Cape Town, Dubai, Hägendorf, Hong Kong,
Indianapolis, Manila, New Delhi, Singapore, Sydney, Tehran, Vienna

 Member of the World Sport Publishers' Association (WSPA)

Total production by: Print Consult GmbH, Germany, Munich
ISBN 978-1-78255-062-4
E-Mail: info@m-m-sports.com
www.m-m-sports.com

TABLE OF CONTENTS

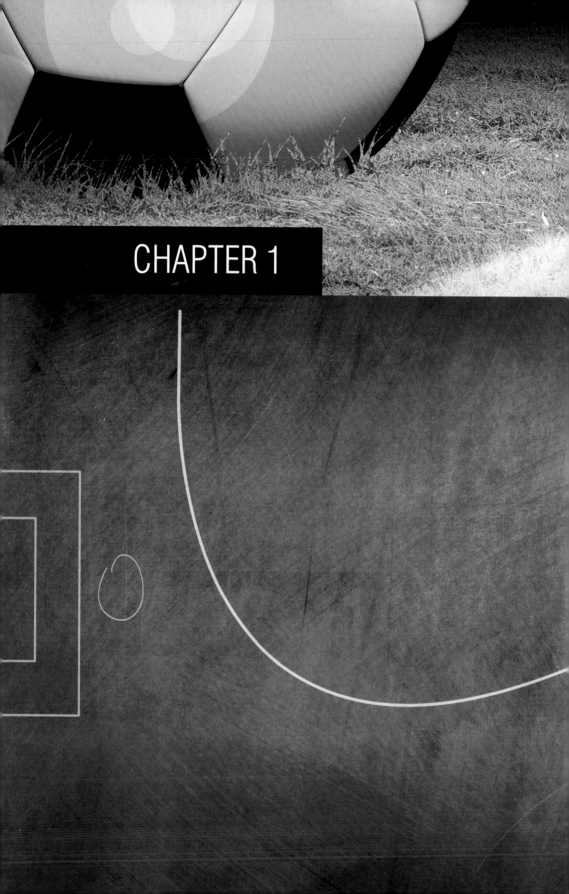

CHAPTER 1

Soccer Starts in the Head

Soccer Starts in the Head

"Soccer always starts in the head, and from there it moves through the body to the feet, never the other way around."

Iniesta demonstrating game intelligence against multiple opponents

Soccer enchants and fascinates people like no other sport does.

Playing accomplished soccer at the highest level depends on many factors, such as athleticism, technique, tactics, game intelligence, mentality, and personality, all of which must be perfectly synchronized.

Any one of these factors alone does not bring success.

What characterizes a good soccer player is the intelligent merging of each of these individual factors to find the optimal solution for each game situation.

By using strategic measures that can be divided into individual, group, and team tactics, these factors can then be transferred to an entire team.

When two teams are evenly matched, in the end it is a good game idea, the right tactics, the appropriate system, and the perfect execution of a plan that emphasize the abilities of each individual player and bring success.

Every soccer magazine and every live soccer broadcast refer to and even depict terms like *tactics, system of play, formations, 1-4-4-3,* and *match plan,* but rarely are they explained in any detail.

Often the significance of these terms is underestimated, because at the end of the day, every success in soccer is the result of training, hard work, and detailed planning.

This funny but true anecdote illustrates the importance of tactical principles in soccer:

A youth coach says to his players: "Today the five of you will play in the back!" One of the young players courageously replies: "Uh, Coach, where exactly is the back and can I occasionally come forward?" The coach replies: "Hmm, good question..."

How are young players supposed to understand the game as a whole without understanding a game idea or tactic?

How are they supposed to learn that an attacker must also switch to defense after a turnover and that a defender gets involved in attacking play during possession?

Even at a young age, tactical themes can be explained in a fun way. Though terms like *tactics* or *switching over* don't need to be mentioned at all, a tactical education process can already begin at a young age.

Throughout the history of soccer, each successful coach has always prepared and organized his team based on tactical considerations and plans, as well as his team's—and the opponents'—strengths and weaknesses, further illustrating the importance of tactics.

Terms, such as the *WM-system (1-3-2-2-3)* created by former Arsenal coach Herbert Chapman and used by Germany in their 1954 World Cup victory, or the *Italian Catenaccio (1-5-4-1)* perfected by Helenio Herrera of Inter Milan, are deeply anchored in soccer history.

The well-known coach and three-time World Cup participant Guus Hiddink is convinced that a trainer should always focus on tactics first, because that is what soccer's performance factors build on.

A coach must always be certain of his game idea and tactical requirements first before he can deduce the appropriate content for his training units.

Successful coach

Guus Hiddink

In soccer, a player is only as good as the next game, which is why a soccer coach always has to think about how to purposefully transfer a game idea and tactical measures to his team in order to win the next game.

Being optimally prepared for every game requires a plan for every single game day—the match plan.

The purpose of this book is to provide anyone who is interested in and enthusiastic about soccer with information on topics such as game idea, tactics, switching play, zone soccer, as well as advantages and disadvantages of various formations based on an analysis of world standards. After reading this book, you can apply these ideas and background knowledge to independently develop a specific match plan for a single game.

Have fun reading and putting it to use!

CHAPTER 2

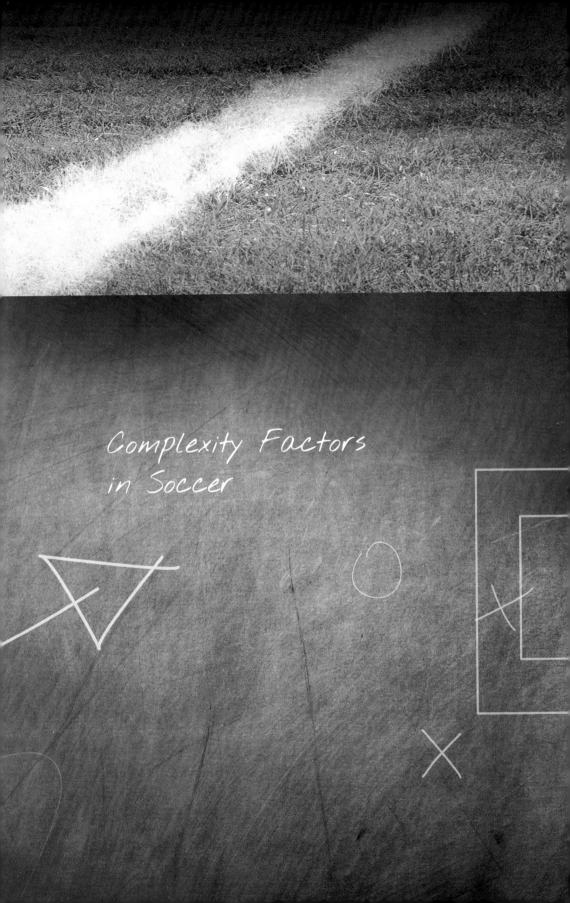

Complexity Factors in Soccer

CHAPTER 2

Complexity Factors in Soccer

"We play best when the opponent isn't there."

Otto Rehhagel, 2004 European Champion with Greece

*F*irst, I will explain the most important factors that make soccer such a complex high-performance sport and that greatly impact tactical considerations.

2.1 FOOT INSTEAD OF HAND

In soccer, the ball is played with the feet rather than the hands, like in basketball or team handball. Playing with the feet greatly increases the number of errors, because even with a perfect technique, the ball cannot be controlled nearly as well as it can with the hands. Because of their everyday use for activities such as writing or eating with a knife and fork, the hands allow for more finesse in sports than the feet do.

2.2 LARGE FIELD AND MANY PLAYERS

Other factors that make soccer a very challenging sport are the large number of players and the large playing field, which for international games must be 105 m long and 68 m wide per FIFA regulations, resulting in a 7140 m² field.

Other team sports, such as team handball, basketball, or ice hockey, have fewer players and play on a smaller field, which creates many more scoring opportunities. So it is not unusual for basketball games to end with three-digit scores and team handball games with double-digit scores.

In soccer, however, a single moment can decide an entire game.

2.3   SMALL GOAL

Soccer originates in rugby. However, in todays' rugby, players can put the ball down by hand behind the entire goal line to score a point on a playing field of roughly equal size, whereas in soccer the ball must be deposited into a 7.32 m x 2.44 m goal that is guarded by the only player who is allowed to use his hands.

2.4   EXTERNAL INFLUENCING FACTORS

External influencing factors, such as weather and the condition of the playing surface, also play a major role. Other team sports like team handball, basketball, or volleyball are played in a gymnasium where the floor is almost always the same and the weather is not a factor.

2.5   DIFFERENT QUALIFICATIONS

In soccer, the coordination of all athletic abilities, such as speed, coordination, strength, endurance, and agility, must be mastered to a degree that hardly any other sport requires. Other sports require an athlete to be well trained in only one of these abilities. In addition, the constant switching back and forth between offense and defense requires a high degree of game intelligence.

2.6   CONCLUSION

It is precisely because of this great complexity as well as a high degree of unpredictability and the many requirements that specific measures are needed to counteract the unpredictability principle in soccer as much as possible and to increase the probability of success.

Thus every coach needs to have a plan if he wants to train purposefully and improve his team.

The following approach would be the opposite and is unfortunately often used by coaches:

"What and how we train isn't that important because almost everything that happens in soccer is coincidental!"

Now ask yourself whether you would like to train with such a coach.

The word *training* in itself suggests that I train systematically and intentionally to improve my performance.

"Every detail matters!"

Top teams can be seen playing recurring game situations that take place remarkably often and can't be a coincidence.

By using the appropriate measures, it is possible for a team to create more scoring opportunities and to prevent the opponent's scoring opportunities with defense.

Passing lanes and running lanes can be optimally synchronized so that exact implementation becomes more important than coincidence.

Standard situations, for instance, can be easily rehearsed and still have a lot of potential in soccer.

And, and, and...

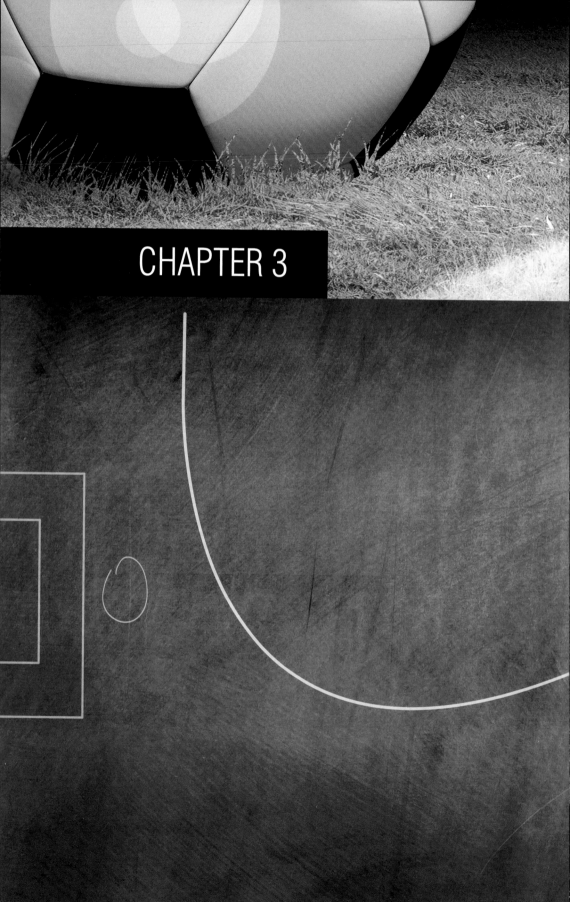

CHAPTER 3

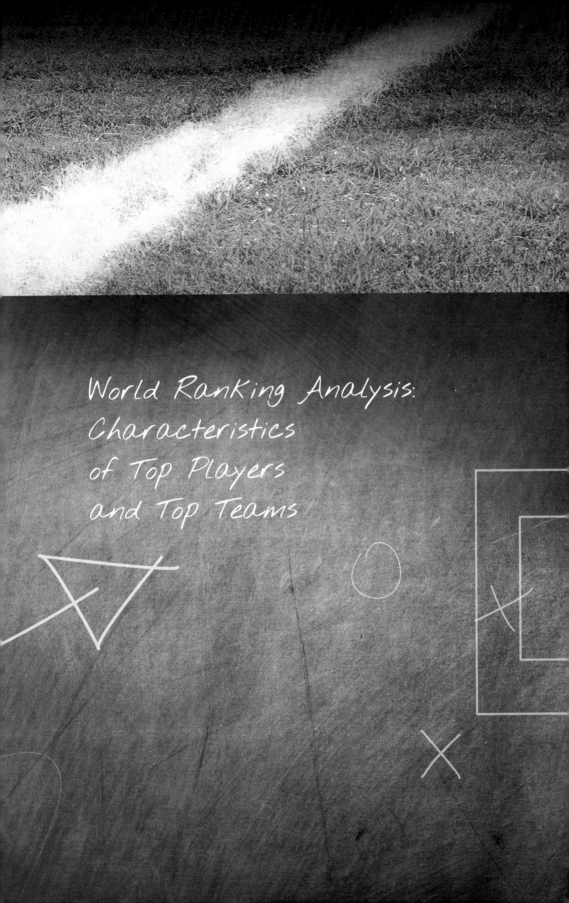

World Ranking Analysis:
Characteristics
of Top Players
and Top Teams

World Ranking Analysis: Characteristics of Top Players and Top Teams

"Look at the best team, learn from the best, be the best!"

Pele, World Player of the 20th century

To begin with, every soccer coach must know what the distinguishing features of the best players and teams are. Only then can a coach develop suitable measures, such as a game idea, and a suitable training philosophy to train players at the highest level and with the highest standards.

Using a world ranking analysis, the best teams from the top international leagues as well as the Champions League, the Continental Championships, and, of course, the World Cups are analyzed and compared in order to make recommendations and to identify developments and trends in elite soccer. The following characteristics distinguish the top teams and top players in modern soccer.

World Champions Germany

3.1   TECHNIQUE

All players, including the goalie, must have had perfect soccer training to be able to master all game situations under extreme pressure from the opponent and time limit.

The players must have perfect basic technical skills on which to build the respective techniques for positional play.

Here the 10,000-hour rule crops up once again. This rule says that it takes 10,000 hours to acquire a complex skill—for instance, a perfect positional playing technique in soccer.

An important point with respect to technique is that ball contact should be as brief as possible. Less ball contact separates the top teams from more average teams.

International top players pass the ball on average after one second!

In addition, the former World Champions Iniesta and Xavi of FC Barcelona immediately pass on nearly every other ball with an extremely high success rate, making it extremely difficult for the opposing team to defend these players because the ball is changing locations every second.

During the 2012 European Championships, 11 out of 16 teams played far more than 500 passes on average per game. This statistic emphasizes the importance of passing play.

Xavi – Perfect technique

European Champion Spain even made an average 847 passes per game with a success rate of more then 80%.

The goal of top teams is to appear as dominant as possible. To that end, it is important to have possession as much as possible.

This requires perfect passing. Because passing is the most common technical element in soccer, it must be mastered with both feet.

Every tenth of a second a teammate gains with an accurate and well-timed pass creates time for better decisions.

Technically perfect inside kick

Compared to other kicks, such as the instep or outside of the foot, the inside kick offers the largest contact area and, therefore, the most accurate execution.

The run-up is straight toward the ball. The supporting leg is slightly bent toward the ball, and the supporting foot is approximately one to two foot-widths away from the ball.

The playing foot is rotated out at an approximately 90-degree angle to the supporting foot. The toe is flexed so that the sole is parallel to the ground. The arms provide balance with the elbows bent at the sides in a natural position.

As with every action, good body tension is important here. The ball must be struck in the center to keep it form bouncing.

3.2   ATHLETICISM

To be able to compete at the highest level, the fitness-related abilities of strength, endurance, speed, coordination, and agility must be perfectly developed and tailored to the specific position requirements.

Throughout soccer's history, players' running ability has greatly increased. Currently a team has to run 71.5 to 78 miles collectively if it wants to play at the highest level.

Elite soccer players run on average more than 7.5 miles per game.

Midfielders and wingbacks cover the most ground.

Mathieu Flamini of Arsenal London holds the European record of more than 9 miles per game.

Even international top-level goalies cover approximately 4 miles per game. The average heart rate for top soccer players who move throughout the game is 160 bpm, which is roughly 80% of maximum oxygen absorption. This clearly attests to the greatly increased intensity at which these games are played.

Even more important than the amount of running is the quality of the running performance.

Soccer has turned into a very intense intermittent serial sprint discipline in which a player has to complete up to 190 sprints per game.

In some cases, top international players run faster than 20.5 mph during a game when sprinting without the ball. This speed is not much slower than 100-m world record holder Usain Bolt, who ran an average 23 mph for his 100-m world record.

Cristiano Ronaldo—perfectly combined technique and athleticism

3.3   MENTAL FACTORS

Any player who takes the field in a lion's den of 80,000 spectators or steps up to take the deciding penalty kick at a World Cup final must be very strong mentally.

Often it is precisely mental strength that determines whether someone makes the leap into pro soccer.

Self-confidence, assertiveness, passion, willingness to take risks, courage, and the desire to succeed are decisive mental factors.

Another important aspect is the player's ability to handle criticism and to bring top performances under extremely high pressure.

More than a few coaches hold the following view:

"Mentality beats quality!"

Only those who won't settle for anything less than the best performance can make it as pro soccer players.

In soccer training it is also extremely important to focus on healthy self-confidence at an early age.

Many coaches even view self-confidence as the most important building block to strive for in training because healthy self-confidence automatically requires the player to be perfectly trained in all aspects of soccer. Only when a player is perfectly trained in all aspects of soccer is he able to have confidence in himself.

In addition, humility and strength of character are important qualities that for many represent the true secret to the success of great teams.

"The game is always bigger than the individual."

"The name on the front is more important than the one on the back."

It's about the ball — not player

3.4   DEFENSE

The ball-oriented game has found worldwide acceptance and is the prevailing basic concept in defensive play.

The foremost objective of defensive play is to move to the ball as a team in a solid block.

Aerial views from the top rows in a stadium show that in highly organized teams this solid block is approximately 27 x 27 yards, which makes it extremely compact.

Simplified image of a compact defensive block

This narrows the opponent's area of action and delays attacks.

There are continuous efforts to create a superior number close to the ball in order to take the ball.

All top teams use targeted defensive strategies to capture the ball as far away as possible from their own goal.

The highest priority after a turnover, and when switching over to defense if counter-pressing is not an option, is to get as many players as possible behind the ball to recapture the ball with a well-organized and closely staggered defense.

Defensive players have improved greatly, particularly with respect to technique, and have consequently gained much appreciation.

In the not-so-distant past, it would have been unthinkable to spend 30 million euros for a defensive player.

However, recently, the two central defenders Rio Ferdinand and Thiago Silva came with a price tag of 40 million euros, which underscores the increased estimation of defensive players.

The most expensive defender overall is David Luiz of the Brazilian national team, who switched from Chelsea London to Paris Saint-Germain in 2014 for the record sum of 49.5 million euros.

Rio Ferdinand—40 million euros for a defensive player

3.5 OFFENSE

In international teams, there has been a definite trend toward more offensive play. In most top teams, the number of players in front of the ball continues to increase.

The main characteristics of modern offensive play are high variability and creativity, as well as perfect positional play.

The team in possession tries to fan out as wide and as deep as possible to counteract the narrowing of the playing field.

Quick switching play forces the opponent to run, and hard vertical balls are used to outplay the opposing lines.

For some time, it has been a trend to field wing players "laterally reversed" so that they can move the ball with the foot that is away from the opponent to the center toward the goal. They can then take a shot with their strong foot from a central position.

Another term that has been surfacing in the media for some time is the *false nine*.

Vicente del Bosque coined the term and used this variation during the 2012 European Championship win. Originally, this term was known as a *variable nine*.

As the name suggests, the variable nine creates high variability in the offense.

It must be noted, though, that the variable nine only works for teams that can stay in possession for long periods of time.

The variable nine continually drops back to center field in order to evade the fullbacks who are often unable to figure out how to handle such a situation.

Using the variable nine means that position 9 is continually freed up and variably occupied by different players.

The FC Barcelona star Cesc Fàbregas did an outstanding job in this role at the 2012 European Championships.

But it must be mentioned that even in the past, players such as the Danish European Champion Michael Laudrup have done a superb job interpreting the false nine.

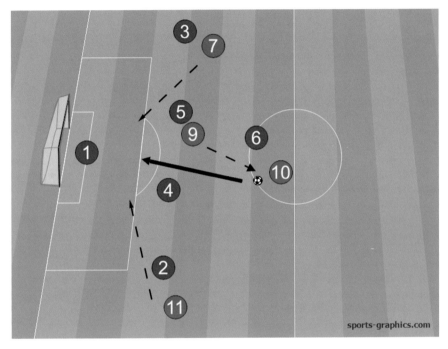

Variable nine

Taking advantage of the opponent's disorganization by using fast, vertical counterattacks with few touches to quickly take a shot on goal is becoming increasingly more important.

The quick execution of a counterattack is very important because top teams are disorganized for only approximately 6 to 10 seconds after a turnover.

As was already mentioned with respect to technique, contact time between ball and foot should be as brief as possible to avoid pressing situations and to quickly take advantage of open spaces.

arsenal drill 7 √5

Additionally, individual abilities will become more important when offensive play decides games.

Exceptionally skilled players like Cristiano Ronaldo, Lionel Messi, Gareth Bale, or Zlatan Ibrahimović are becoming more expensive and more important since often only a single action or a masterstroke can punch holes in the opposing defense.

Exceptionally skilled player, Zlatan Ibrahimović

3.6   PACE

In soccer, the pace of the game has undergone the biggest change.

When looking at a list of the current best players in the world, it is apparent that all of them are able to play at a fast pace, when dribbling, sprinting into open space, or even executing a brilliant pass.

To Louis van Gaal, speed is also a tactical tool that must used correctly in the situation.

Players require good action ability because they must make and execute the right decisions in a fraction of a second, and they have less and less space and time to do so when the game moves at such a fast pace.

Switching play is extremely important and will continue to be one of the decisive key points as the pace continues to get faster.

Fast counter-pressing is another trend in soccer. The change in the back-pass rule in 1990 has laid the foundation for this tactical tool.

In the past, after a turnover, teams tried to form a compact team unit behind the ball as quickly as possible.

Today, world-class teams like Bayern Munich or FC Barcelona try to quickly win back the ball within five seconds.

Along with creating shorter distance to the opposing goal, another benefit of counter-pressing is that it takes advantage of the opponent's disorganization.

You can Counter-press w/ speed — especially in their defending 1/3

3.7 THE 1-0 LEAD

The number of goals scored continues to decline, particularly during the World Cups. At the World Cup in Korea in 2002, 161 goals were scored.

Eight years later, at the World Cup in South Africa, there were only 145 goals.

Though the number of goals continues to decrease, soccer training theory continues to advance. Consequently, nearly all teams at the World Cup and in the Champions League are exceptionally well organized, particularly in the area of defense.

This continually raises and equalizes the *niveau* of soccer teams, which is why today it matters more than ever which team is in the lead.

3.8 HEADERS

The current best offensive and defensive header Sergio Ramos of Real Madrid first took Bayern Munich out of the 2013/2014 Champions League tournament in the semi-final with two headers, and in the final against Atletico Madrid, he brought victory with a header goal in extra time. Incidentally, in this Champions League final, the first three goals were all headers.

In the context of standard situations, there has been a very definite trend toward headers in soccer, demonstrating their significance. The 2012 European Championships affirmed their great importance:

* 22 of 76 goals were scored with a header!

Fewer and fewer players will be able to succeed without perfect header play.

In 2006, Zinedine Zidane led France to the World Cup final with two header goals. Cristiano Ronaldo's header skills are well-known, and even the five-foot-six Lionel Messi clinched the 2011 Champions League final with a fantastic header goal.

Lionel Messi with a tremendous header in the Champions League final against Manchester United

Even for dominant teams that play with low crosses, such as FC Barcelona, header play is becoming increasingly important, as many opponents use high balls as a counterattack that must be defended against.

Mats Hummels—skilled header

CHAPTER 4

2014 World Champions:
The German National
Soccer Team's
Match Plan

2014 World Champions: The German National Soccer Team's Match Plan

Germany—Worthy World Champions 2014

*A*ll the experts agree:

The German national soccer team deserves the Word Championship title because Germany fielded the most flawless and most compact team of the 24 participating nations.

While runners-up Argentina also presented a cohesive unit, offensively the team was too dependent on the individual strengths of Messi and Di María—who got injured during the semi-final match.

Without a doubt, the coach of the German team, Joachim Löw, deserves much of the credit for the 2014 World Cup win in Brazil.

Because he put together the right combination of players, used optimal preparation, created perfectly designed match plans, and provided the proper motivation, Joachim Löw is the coach of the 2014 World Cup.

4.1 THE 10 SUCCESS FACTORS AND TRENDS OF THE 2014 WORLD CUP

Many modern soccer trends were confirmed and advanced during the Brazil World Cup.

The following are the 10 most significant development trends observed at the Brazil World Cup.

 ### 1. GREAT TACTICAL VARIABILITY

At the 2010 World Cup in South Africa, many teams still played in a rigid 1-4-2-3-1 formation.

Nearly every soccer formation could be seen at the Brazil World Cup.

Whether it was 1-4-3-3, 1-3-4-3, 1-5-4-1, 1-4-4-2, or 1-4-3-1-2, nearly every formation possible was used.

Many teams were even able to change their formations multiple times during a game, confirming a high degree of tactical variability.

You may switch formations during a match

World Champion Germany also used different formations and easily switched them during a game.

Some teams, like Ecuador or Croatia, exhibited rather static tactical play, but it was obvious that allegedly "smaller" teams have made enormous tactical strides and were able to trump their opponent's individual playing level. Costa Rica was certainly a prime example.

It was confirmed at the World Cup that a fixed order no longer exists. Rather, an offensive and a defensive order exists that varies depending on the opponent and the game situation.

Soccer coaches must, therefore, be extremely tactically variable.

German soccer head instructor and U-20 coach Frank Wormuth has this to say on the subject:

"In the future, all coaches must have mastery of every system and be able to change the formation as needed. Given these requirements the head coaches must be even more careful when working out the lineup."

2. STRATEGIC FLEXIBILITY

Next to a high degree of tactical variability, the top teams also had the ability to change their strategy.

Germany, for example, varied its strategy between purposeful possession play and a form of compact, surprise counterattack soccer.

The top teams also used different strategies with respect to pressing and were able to change their pressing strategies within a game as well.

If—then strategies were also often skillfully employed—in cases of a point deficit or a red card, for instance.

The perfect example for this was Germany in the World Cup final. First Sami Khedira had to be replaced on short notice, and then Christoph Kramer, who had replaced

Khedira without a problem, had to be replaced after only 30 minutes because of an injury. After this, Germany changed its formation.

When Louis van Gaal replaced his starting goalie Cillessen with the penalty kick expert Krul just before the end of extra time in the quarter-final against Costa Rica, it was a stroke of genius.

Krul held the decisive penalty kick and made van Gaal a hero.

Louis van Gaal and penalty kick expert Tim Krul—a replacement that was a strategic stroke of genius

3. THE COMEBACK OF THE THREE-MAN AND THE FIVE-MAN BACKLINE AS THE DEFENSIVE SYSTEM OF THE FUTURE

The comeback of the three-man backline has long been seen in club soccer, and it is currently being used by many teams for offensive formation, particularly.

An extremely compact five-man backline during defensive play was a sweeping and tried-and-tested trend at the World Cup.

It is no coincidence that more and more teams are using a five-man backline on defense in reaction to the opponents' increasingly complex offensives.

Of note: The Netherlands as well as Costa Rica, who played primarily with a five-man backline, did not lose a single game in normal time.

The major advantages of the five-man backline:

- No gaps: Even when a player leaves the five-man backline, four players still remain.
- Players can run up to the opponent's most important players in all zones, allowing for better control of the space between the five-man backline and the midfield.

Costa Rica perfectly implemented the five-man backline.

The Costa Rican five-man line moved toward the ball together in a line. When the wingback pressed forward, the remaining players in the five-man line pushed up and covered the spaces at consistent distances, making it nearly impossible for the opponent to break through.

Look up the 5 man back line

Costa Rica

Costa Rica—convincing with team spirit and a five-man backline

4. MUST HAVES: FAST SWITCHING PLAY AND STANDARD SITUATIONS

The ability to quickly switch play during the fourth game phase was THE guarantee for success at the World Cup.

In addition, 30% of all goals at the World Cup were scored after standard situations.

Standard situations, in particular, still hold enormous potential, because what coach invests 30% of his time in penalty kicks, free kicks, corners, or throw-ins?!

The best remedy against standard situations is to not ever let them happen.

When choosing his players, Joachim Löw made sure that they would be able to play without committing fouls and avoid unforced errors near the penalty area.

And if standard situations should still occur, excellent head ball players such as Mats Hummels, Jerome Boateng, or Per Mertesacker are needed, especially for corners and standards from the half space.

An outstanding goalie like Manuel Neuer is needed for direct and indirect free kicks near the penalty area.

The German team ranked at the top for defensive as well as offensive standards, particularly in the standard situations category.

5. MORE MAN-TO-MAN DEFENSE

Many teams, such as the Netherlands, use targeted man-to-man defense despite the prevalent zone defense.

Chile and Algeria, for example, had phases of nearly exclusive man-to-man defense during their aggressive pressing.

This man-to-man defense is used to force 1v1 situations, which attests to the ever increasing individual skill level, with the attempt to prevent these through very specific assignment.

6. FLEXIBLE INTERPRETATION OF THE WINGBACK ROLE

The interpretation of the wingback role varied greatly during this World Cup.

Though the wingbacks focused primarily on nearly exclusive wing play at the last World Cup, the tactical interpretation was significantly greater at this World Cup.

The Brazilian player Marcelo, for example, who started as left back for Brazil, also periodically took on the role of playmaker during offensive play.

German national team captain Philipp Lahm—world-class central midfielder and wingback

Kuyt of the Netherlands played this position with incredible unpredictability and at times—depending on the opponent—even in the half space.

Germany occasionally played with two trained central defenders as wingbacks. Consequently, the wingback positions had a rather more defensive interpretation.

And, of course, the exceptional Philipp Lahm, who is an absolute world-class player in his usual position as wingback as well as central midfielder, cannot be overlooked.

7.   THE GOALIE'S ENORMOUS REQUIREMENT PROFILE

The goalie has made the permanent transition from goalkeeper to goal player.

At the 2014 World Cup, the goalie position was manned with the strongest players.

Whether it was Manuel Neuer, Keylor Navas, Claudio Bravo, Tim Howard, Hugo Lloris, Jasper Cillessen, or Sergio Romero, all teams possessed a goalie with a tremendous individual skill level.

The paradigm was Manuel Neuer's performance against Algeria during the round of 16.

Paradigm of a modern goal player—Manuel Neuer's tackle against Algeria

8.   RETURN OF THE ATTACKING FORWARD AND THE SIGNIFICANCE OF THE FALSE 9

As was apparent in the World Cup, the attacking forward will continue to become more relevant against increasingly better-organized defensive blocks.

On the German team, for instance, the top World Cup scorer Miroslav Klose played a very significant role in this capacity.

Flexibility in offensive play is necessary and crucial. The false 9 can greatly contribute to offensive flexibility.

Mario Götze was brought on as a false 9 to substitute for attacking forward Miroslav Klose and scored the decisive goal for the German team in the World Cup final.

Mario Götze scoring the winning goal as a false 9

9.   TEAM SPIRIT AND SUPER-SUB GOALS:
     SUBSTITUTE PLAYERS IN THE WORLD CUP

Everyone knows that soccer is a team sport, but never has team spirit been expressed as emphatically as during the 2014 World Cup.

Players from South American teams such as Chile, Columbia, or Costa Rica practically knocked themselves out for their teammates.

Team spirit—the World Cup of super-subs

The German squad's great team spirit was convincing.

In addition, more goals were scored by super-subs at the 2014 World Cup than ever before; 31 of 171 goals were scored by subs, which speaks volumes.

10. DIGRESSION:

The Planned Bad Pass as a Tactical Resource

It is common knowledge that a high percentage of goals are scored immediately after a turnover. This also was very apparent at the Brazil World Cup.

In club soccer, Borussia Dortmund, under Jürgen Klopp, is setting new standards in this area with a perfect counter-pressing.

It is, therefore, no longer surprising that the use of the planned bad pass as a tactical strategy is a topic of discussion.

Attractive, fast-paced offensive soccer is made increasingly difficult by more compact and tactically-perfect defensive blocks.

It is, therefore, worth more than just a consideration to purposefully cede the ball to the opposing team in certain situations for the purpose of winning the ball with a pre-arranged counter-press and exploiting the opponent's lack of defensive structure.

This consideration is of particular interest with regard to throw-ins because here the options for continuing play are very limited and spaces are easily blocked.

Statistics confirm throwing the ball into touch during the own team's throw-in and then blocking is often more promising than just doing a throw-in.

Match Plan: The Journey of the German National Team

With his match plans, World Champion coach Joachim Löw managed to eliminate the random principle as much as possible.

Being able to figure out and exploit the opponent's game strategy creates a major advantage when entering the battle between coaches.

By having elaborate match plans, detailed opponent analyses, and accurate appraisals that were then perfectly implemented on the field by the German national team, the German squad was superbly attuned to its opponents throughout the entire tournament.

GROUP STAGE

GERMANY VS PORTUGAL 4-0

Germany countered the Portuguese 1-4-3-3 formation with their own 1-4-3-3.

This was Joachim Löw's reaction to the opponent, which was particularly apparent in his choice of players.

Foul with consequences—Portuguese defender Pepe hits Müller and sees red

Thus the backline of four was manned with four central defenders to counter the high individual skill level of Cristiano Ronaldo and Nani on the wings with increased defensive stability.

Löw's match plan was successful.

What was eyed critically by the press turned out to be a key success factor in this game.

On offense, Germany's interpretation of the 1-4-3-3 was much more flexible and also prevailed because of the overall better individual skill level, as is so often the case when two identical systems of play encounter each other.

In addition, Mats Hummels scored from a rehearsed standard situation with a fantastic header.

GERMANY VS GHANA 2-2

Joachim Löw analyzed the game against Ghana as follows: "The first half was very tactical; the second half was a slugfest, which we really tried to avoid. Two goals came out of nowhere; but then our team rallied very nicely."

The German squad's lead from Götze initially confirmed a match plan of lots of possession play but was promptly equalized with a nice header by Ayew, during which Mustafi, who had come into the game at half-time for Boateng, did not look good.

Then Gyan was able to turn a rare bad pass from Lahm into the lead.

This resulted in the outright slugfest previously cited by Löw.

The extreme climate conditions caused the running performance and the compactness to diminish.

But Germany had to play more offensively, which created more spaces for Ghana's dangerous counterattacks, and Ghana absolutely needed to win this game.

But then Germany managed to score the well-deserved equalizer from a corner that was extended by Höwedes to the second post where Klose was perfectly positioned.

Ghana celebrates the leading goal against the eventual World Champions.

USA VS GERMANY 0-1

The German team won their group with a 1-0 victory over the USA.

This win speaks to the tremendous winning mentality and attitude of the German team, who had already qualified for the round of 16 before this game.

The German defense was noticeable stronger than against Ghana. Germany allowed the USA team a total of only four shots on goal.

Old friends—Klinsmann and Löw after the game

Germany's midfield controlled the game and dominated with high possession (67%). USA resisted with compact pressing and good shifting play.

Of note:

The winning goal once again resulted from a standard situation.

Thomas Müller scored the well-deserved winning goal with a deliberate inside foot kick after a short corner variation.

ROUND OF 16

GERMANY VS ALGERIA 2-1 AET

Defensively, Germany played in a 1-4-4-2 to avoid running into one of Algeria's dangerous counterattacks. Offensively, they played in their usual 1-4-3-3.

Germany struggled against Algeria's aggressive man-to-man defense but kept their calm in this game, too. Germany won, thanks again to an outstanding Manuel Neuer.

Manuel Neuer's heat map (an image of the field showing players' positions during the game) of this game very clearly shows the performance of a modern goalie.

The preplanned substitution of Andre Schürrle as the new outside right decided the game.

Squawka Football ✓
@Squawka

⚙ 👤 Follow

Here it is, the most talked about heat map in history. Manuel Neuer. #GER ○

↩ ↻ ★ ⋯

RETWEETS 1,777   FAVORITES 954

12:47 AM · 1 Jul 2014

Manuel Neuer's heat map (all rights reserved by Squawka)

Schürrle continuously positioned himself high and wide and kept looking for the 1v1, exploiting the defensive weaknesses of his offensively strong opposing player, Ghoulam.

Germany had to fight against a strong Algerian team, and the German team's performance was met with excessive criticism.

First of all, there are no weak opponents at the round of 16 of a World Cup, and in the end, with 28-10 shots on goal, 66% possession, and 56% of duels won, the statistics reflect a deserved victory.

QUARTER-FINAL

FRANCE VS GERMANY 0-1

Against a tough French team, Germany played without Per Mertesacker, and for the first time, Joachim Löw put in team captain Lahm as wingback.

This change was necessary to optimally counter the versatile Benzema of Real Madrid.

Bastian Schweinsteiger was impressive as the organizer in the central midfield, and Philipp Lahm gave a very strong performance in his usual position.

Miroslav Klose started for Mario Götze, allowing Thomas Müller to start in his preferred position on the right outside lane.

The German lineup was well prepared for the strong French team, and Mats Hummels scored the winning goal once again from a standard situation rehearsed in a match plan.

Mats Hummels "using his head" for the winning goal once again after a standard situation

SEMI-FINAL

BRAZIL VS GERMANY 1-7

As against Portugal and France, the German team was able to immediately stifle Brazil's build-up play with rehearsed pressing.

During the first half, Germany's disciplined shifting to the ball allowed them to win nearly every second ball. In addition, they were able to isolate Brazil's offense by outnumbering them.

Unbelievable—7-1 Germany vs Brazil

In addition to pressing geared at the opponents, Brazil's weakness in shifting play was ruthlessly exploited.

Germany took the lead with yet another rehearsed standard by Thomas Müller, followed by another goal by Miroslav Klose, who became World Cup record holder with this goal.

Within seven minutes, Germany expanded their lead to 5-0, and with that, the game was decided after only half an hour.

Löw then changed the system to 1-4-2-3-1 for the final phase of the game. Özil switched to the 10 role, and Germany's defense remained very compact and was able to save crucial strength for the final.

FINAL

GERMANY VS ARGENTINA 1-0 AET

Never change a winning team. Keeping in mind this well-known truth, Germany and Argentina intended to compete with the same lineup as in the semi-finals.

But just before the start of the game Sami Khedira had to drop out during the warm-up.

However, a good match plan takes into account unforeseen circumstances like this, so Christoph Kramer moved up into the starting lineup.

The way Germany handled the last-minute loss of Khedira was impressive, which is a sign of quality and evidence of a strong team mindset.

As with previous games, Joachim Löw again relied on the 1-4-3-3, and Argentina's coach Alejandro Sabella stuck with his compact 1-4-4-1-1 to create lots of openings for superstar Lionel Messi, who operated behind the versatile Gonzalo Higuaín.

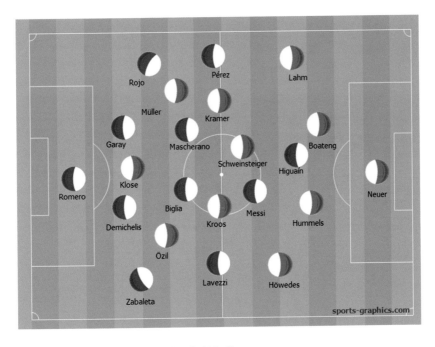

Formation in the 2014 World Cup final at the kick-off

GERMANY 1-4-3-3 VS ARGENTINA 1-4-4-1-1

As in every game, on offense, Argentina tried to operate with the "Messi concept," but the German squad was well prepared for this and tried to counteract every touch with the appropriate safeguard. Of course, this strategy was not 100% effective against such a skilled player. Thus, Messi initiated some good plays for the Argentinians and created space for his teammates.

Kramer's injury after only half an hour was also handled well by the German team.

Christoph Kramer, last-minute addition to the starting lineup, was injured.

Andre Schürrle came in for Christoph Kramer, changing the 1-4-3-3 to a 1-4-2-3-1.

Mesut Özil hustled in his preferred position in the central offensive midfield, Schürrle played on the left wing, and Bastian Schweinsteiger together with Toni Kroos safeguarded on the double six.

Operating with such immense tactical versatility had been inconceivable at the beginning of the Löw era.

In the second half, Sabella adjusted his team and played in a 1-4-3-1-2 diamond, which Germany initially had trouble adjusting to. Löw made the strategically-wise decision to reposition his players.

Kroos moved from the double six up one position next to Özil, creating a 1-4-1-4-1, making Germany once again dominant in the midfield and, with 64%, clearly the team with the most possession in the game.

With the final whistle, the World Champions had run six miles more than Argentina, which is indicative of perfect planning and implementation in the athletic area.

Germany won 54% of all duels and, especially in extra time, was the more active team. Germany continued to pursue their quest while Argentina became passive and kept pulling farther back.

A moment between superstars—Bastian Schweinsteiger consoles Lionel Messi

4.2 THE GERMAN WORLD CHAMPION TEAM'S SECRETS TO SUCCESS

World Champion coach Joachim Löw implemented his match plan successfully

General characteristics

- Dominant in all four game phases
- High tactical variability
- Goal-oriented combination soccer combined with strong 1v1 situations
- World Cup squad with enormous individual skill levels (what other team could leave Götze or Schürrle on the bench, or not even nominate Barcelona goalie Stegen?)
- Highly professional training and coaching staff with experts from all areas
- Enormous team spirit, good morale, and winner mentality
- Mental strength: players with courage, confidence, and lots of self-initiative

Defense

- Purposeful pressing strategies: perfectly rehearsed midfield pressing with fluid transition to forechecking and deeper staggering, based on the situation
- Defensive patterns that are geared to the opponent, depending on the situation
- Extremely well-organized and compact defensive block with close distances
- Participation with major engagement of all players in defense
- Immediate collective counter-pressing after a turnover
- Manuel Neuer as outstanding goalie of the tournament

Offense

- Goal-oriented start of the game with patterns geared to the opponent
- Quick shift in play after gaining possession
- Rapid ball circulation with few touches
- Several vertical short passes into the opponent's seams
- Variable play: lots of position changes in width and depth
- Individual skills in 1v1 duels
- Top skills during offensive standard situations

CHAPTER 5

Game Concept

CHAPTER 5

Game Concept

"Never in my life have I played a game that ended in a tie."

Alex Ferguson, 13-time English Championships winner and two-time Champions League winner

*O*nce you understand the demands of playing with the world's top teams, the next step is to develop a game concept.

All tactical measures always come from a game concept and from which a training philosophy is then derived.

Building on this devised game concept, technical and tactical principles, appropriate systems of play, as well as a goal-oriented training philosophy can then be identified in a subsequent step.

Other terms, like playing philosophy or a coach's script, essentially mean the same thing as game concept.

Every coach must have a definite plan as to how he wants to play soccer.

Every team, every club, every association that plans long-term must develop and internalize its own game concept, because that is what gives a team its identity and allows a club to design a long-term, systematic path.

Many clubs or associations now even make their principles of play public on their webpage or in official documents.

Because only when a game concept has been made public can suitable players be recruited and trained to implement that game concept.

Thus, in one of the world's best clubs, FC Barcelona, the game concept far outranks the tactical focus.

Regardless of whether a junior team or the pros from FC Barcelona are playing, regardless of whether the formation is 1-4-3-3 or 1-3-6-1, the game concept of the tiki-taka (or in Spanish, *tiqui-taca*)—characterized by dominance in all four game phases, long possession times with quick ball circulation, and aggressive counter-pressing—will always be the same and is instilled in the youth players at La Masia from the very start.

La Masia—FC Barcelona's world-famous youth soccer academy

When creating a game concept that will also be incorporated long-term into the youth program, it is important to take into account cultural and local background, such as a country's soccer history and club traditions, for example, since these can have a major impact on a game concept.

The proud, offensive Catalans would never settle for defensive soccer based on counterattacks.

They like to set the tone and be dominant.

In comparison, a game concept in a former Eastern bloc country would, for cultural reasons, rather put more emphasis on good organization and athleticism and most likely never include as much creativity, joy of playing, and open spaces as in an African or South American country.

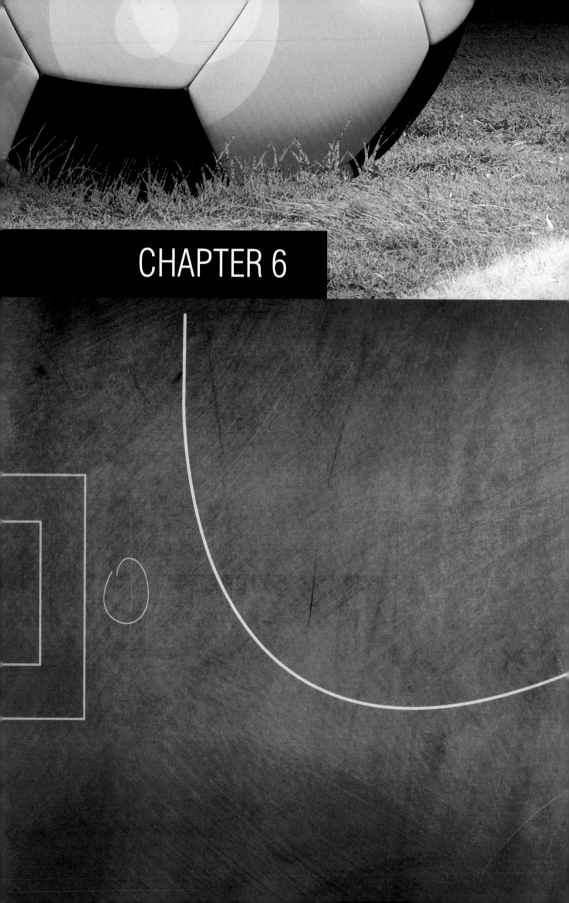

CHAPTER 6

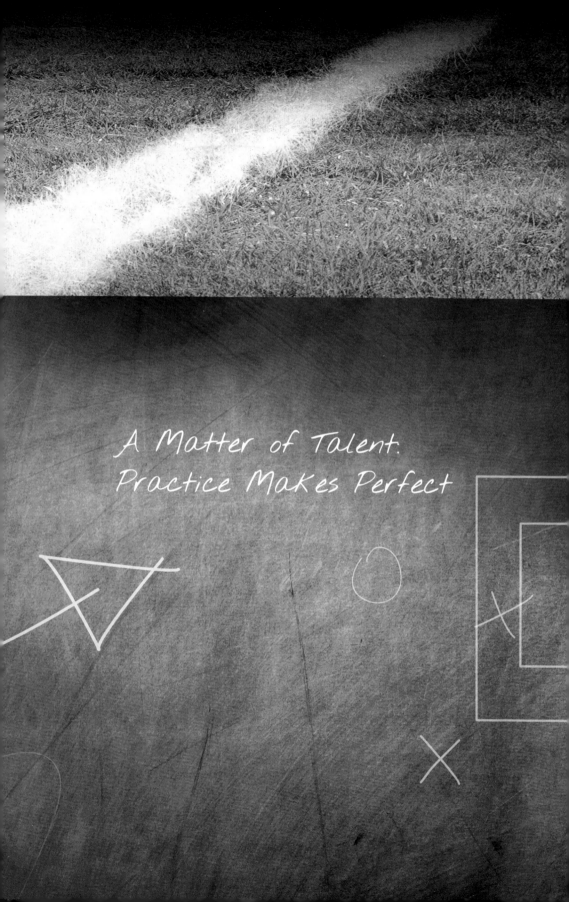

A Matter of Talent.
Practice Makes Perfect

A Matter of Talent: Practice Makes Perfect

"My secret is practice. I have always believed that in order to achieve something special in life one must work for it, work, and work some more."

David Beckham (Champions League winner, Intercontinental Cup winner, and 115 international games played for England)

In order to select the right players for a game concept, the definition of a talent must first be clarified.

Can any human being in good health make it to the professional level or is this something only a special group of people with innate abilities is able to achieve?

Many scientists refer to a talent myth and assert that anyone can become an expert in his field when the right factors come together.

PRACTICE, PRACTICE, PRACTICE

We keep hearing about the 10,000-hour rule made famous by the Swedish psychologist K. Anders Ericsson, who has been thoroughly exploring the subject of talent for two decades.

This rule indicates that it takes 10,000 hours of practice to make it to the top of one's field.

10,000 hours: That would mean 2 hours and 44 minutes of practice every day for 10 years.

Were Amadeus Mozart, Tiger Woods, and Lionel Messi truly child prodigies or was it the fact that these individuals had already practiced for thousands of hours at a very young age?

Mozart, for instance, had already completed more than 3,500 practice hours by age six—an amount of practice even very competent adult musicians don't achieve.

Andre Agassi, one of the world's top tennis players and proclaimed child prodigy, made the following statement in his autobiography Open: "My father says that if I hit 2,500 balls every day, that's 17,500 per week, and at the end of the year nearly a million. Math is his religion. He says that numbers never lie. A child that hits a million balls a year will be invincible."

Ericsson's projection was seized upon by the Hungarian educational psychologist László Polgár, who forged his three daughters into world-class chess players with 10,000 hours of practice, known in professional circles as the "Polgár sisters experiment."

Polgár was convinced that exceptional performance was based on practice. His motto was "Geniuses are made, not born!"

His oldest daughter, Susan, already rose to the number one ranking in the world at the age of 15 and became a four-time winner of the women's world championships.

His daughter, Sofia, already took first place at the Hungarian U-11 championships at age five and won several gold medals at the chess Olympiads.

His youngest daughter, Judith, became grand master at age 15 and is considered the best female chess player of all time. She has defeated male grand masters like Garry Kasparov.

This caused such a sensation that the Dutch billionaire Joop van Oosterom asked Polgár if he would be willing to adopt three children from developmental countries to definitively prove his experiment, but Polgár's wife, however, was not willing to do this.

ENTHUSIASM AND COMMITMENT

It is not just quantity that is important, but also quality of practice. The key is targeted practice that presupposes the individual in question has freely chosen to practice out of an inner motivation and practices with enthusiasm. This inner motivation verifiably activates the necessary areas of the brain more effectively than in a person who does not practice with enthusiasm.

THE RIGHT ENVIRONMENT

In addition to the 10,000 hours of targeted practice, access to the right training opportunities is also important.

The fact that no world champion swimmers hail from Ivory Coast is no surprise since there are no swimming pools there that would make training even possible.

But there are many world-class soccer players from Ivory Coast, such as Didier Drogba or the Touré brothers, which is not surprising since in Abidjan alone more than 3,000 soccer games are played on any given Sunday afternoon.

ENDURANCE

When asked about the most important secret to his success, the great British statesman Winston Churchill replied:

"Never, never, never give up!"

On her way to her Olympic championship title, figure skater Shizuka Arakawa fell more than 20,000 times.

The basketball legend Michael Jordan reported that he missed more than 9,000 throws, and Gerd Müller went down in German soccer history not only as the player with the highest strike rate, but also the most missed shots.

The desire to persevere and not get discouraged by setbacks is also an extremely important feature of an athlete who wants to make it all the way to the top.

DATE OF BIRTH

A remarkable number of soccer players are born in the first quarter of the year. Consequently, they are often further along in their physical development and already have more practice time under their belts, benefitting more from support programs.

The result is that a player receives better training with better teammates and gets more playing time.

In addition, he is praised more often, which gives him more motivation and recognition, boosting his self-confidence.

Therefore, when selecting young players, their date of birth should always be taken into consideration.

EFFORT

Another interesting study was done by Dr. Carol Dweck.
Dweck gave 400 11-year-olds puzzles to assemble.

After the children completed the puzzles, half of them were praised with the words, "You are very talented!" and the other group with the words, "You worked very hard!"

During the next step, the children were asked whether they would choose a more difficult test that would teach them more or a simpler test like the first one.

Astonishingly, more than two-third of the children who had been praised for their talent wanted to take an easier test, while 90% of the children who had been praised for their effort chose the more difficult version.

The group that was praised for their effort was not interested in success but rather in maxing out their potential, while the group who had been praised for their talent did not want to lose their status.

Next the children were given such difficult tasks that none of them were able to solve them. The children who had been praised for their intelligence gave up much quicker and did not consider themselves smart enough to master the problems, and this diminished their self-confidence. The children who were praised for their effort worked significantly longer on their tasks, enjoyed the difficult problems, and continued to have good self-confidence.

Finally, all 400 children completed another test as difficult as the first puzzle.

The talented group's performance declined by 20%, and the group that was praised for their effort improved by 30%.

In sports, the arguably most well-known tennis coach Nick Bollettieri uses this principle in his tennis academy, which has produced many international tennis stars like Andre Agassi and Anna Kournikova.

Bollettieri never praises the talent, only the effort of his students. After a while, this method gives his students a completely different attitude.

The students learn the importance of discipline, hard work, and personal responsibility. Without these values, no athlete would make it to the top.

CONCLUSION

The following aspects must be transferred to soccer and should absolutely be taken into account when selecting and developing young soccer players. Doing so increases the chances for a successful career tremendously:

- Inner motivation: joy, fun, enthusiasm
- 10,000 hours of targeted practice
- Praising effort, not talent
- Taking into account birth date and biological age
- The coach, or rather the player's surroundings, then has the task of offering the players an optimal training environment and accompanying the players on their path, so players can evolve as soccer players as well as individuals.

CHAPTER 7

Tactical Periodization
as a Model
for Modern Training Design

Tactical Periodization as a Model for Modern Training Design

"To learn to play the piano, the piano player doesn't run around the piano, he plays the piano."

DR. MANUEL SÉRGIO

*O*nce a coach and a club develop a game concept, the next question becomes how this game concept can be practiced and implemented so that it can be transported to the playing field.

Taking a look at international soccer in recent years, it is very clear that coaches who work with the *tactical periodization method* are extremely successful and even praised for their playing style.

Portuguese Vitor Frade, who taught soccer at Porto University and was active at FC Porto, developed the tactical periodization model in the 1980s.

The concept of tactical periodization became known in the soccer world primarily through his two students, the successful Portuguese coach André Villas-Boas—who when he was young was able to win the UEFA Cup with FC Porto—and through José

Mourinho—who won multiple Champions League titles.

The tactical periodization model: well-known supporters José Mourinho and André Villas-Boas

Tactical periodization is a *dynamic system concept* and follows a holistic approach.

This means that a soccer player is viewed as a total system that has to combine many different performance factors.

Traditional training theory in which individual performance techniques are often practiced independently of other techniques is outdated, according to the tactical periodization principle. Traditional training theory has been adopted primarily by individual sports such as track and field, so it is not appropriate for soccer training.

A soccer player must always be able to combine different performance factors.

To play successful soccer, technical, tactical, and athletic aspects must be combined with game intelligence and a good tactical perception.

The objective of tactical periodization is to make training as practically relevant and game-like as possible.

In doing so, the ball is the focus of the action in every drill.

In the words of Raymond Verheijen, the expert for soccer-specific fitness training:

"Soccer fitness is obtained by playing soccer!"

The game is the foundation for the tactical periodization model, meaning, the game provides the training.

Therefore, all soccer performance skills are practiced together.

By practicing all skills together, tactics are at the center of training design, because only through tactics can other performance factors like technique or athleticism be carried over from training into a soccer game.

The goal of tactical periodization is to conceptualize the game concept implementation.

Here a clear concept is created from a blend of strategic, tactical as well as training and sports scientific findings, which reflects the basic tactical principles of the game concept.

Tactical periodization divides the game into four phases (see p. 93), and practice drills are designed to include the four key elements: athleticism, technique, psychology, and tactics. Of these four, tactics are always considered the most important.

At the heart of this philosophy, as mentioned in the previous chapter, lies a game concept that is predetermined by the coach or club.

The game concept carries the coach's fingerprints and ideally reflects the coach's vision of how he wants to play soccer on the field.

Another feature of tactical periodization is the significant shortening of training design periodization cycles.

With respect to content, this model requires high game-like intensity of the individual units. This intensity is, however, lowered toward the end of the season.

Also using the tactical periodization concepts: Olympic champion Marcelo Bielsa and Bayern Munich coach Pep Guardiola

Due to the successes of many great coaches, such as the pioneer Marcelo Bielsa of Athlético Bilbao and also Pep Guardiola, who have successfully applied this principle for a long time, the tactical periodization model continues to become more popular.

To some extent, clubs like FC Barcelona and many top South American teams have been using an approach for many years that builds on the principles of tactical periodization.

CHAPTER 8

Tactics

CHAPTER 8

Tactics

"Behind each kick of the ball there must be a thought."

Dennis Bergkamp—former player on the Dutch national team and Arsenal London star, now assistant coach at Ajax Amsterdam

*T*he general term *tactic* originates from the Greek *taktiké* and loosely translated means *arrangement*.

Just like the game concept, tactics in soccer must be goal oriented, with the objective of winning the game.

Meaning: The purpose of tactics in soccer is to optimally implement the soccer game concept, namely to score goals and prevent goals.

Soccer experts agree: The higher the skill level of the opposing teams, the more important the tactical aspect becomes, as the average skill levels of individual players continue to become more equal.

The fact that enormous sums are being paid for exceptionally skilled players proves that theory, because the few exceptional players are very rare and often can make all the difference when two teams play at a near equal level. That is why these exceptional players are so expensive.

Exceptionally-skilled player Gareth Bale—100 million euro transfer fee

But because only a few teams are able to spend that much money on a player or have superior individual players within their ranks, appropriate tactical measures are primarily employed in an effort to gain an edge over the opponent and thereby win the game.

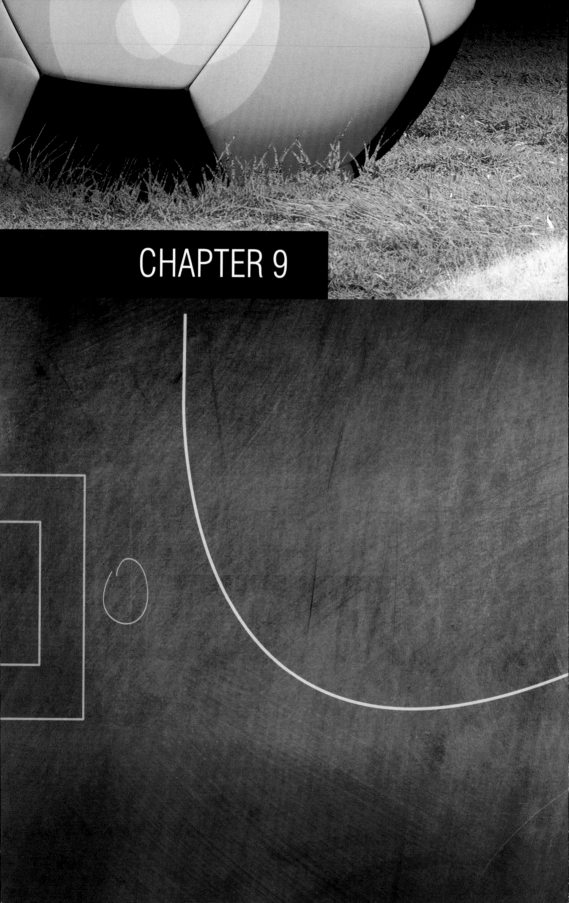

CHAPTER 9

Tactical Actions
in Soccer

CHAPTER 9

Tactical Actions in Soccer

First, soccer tactics can be divided into three areas:

- Individual tactics
- Group tactics
- Team tactics

The specific application of these three areas in a game is called game tactics.

9.1 INDIVIDUAL TACTICS

Individual tactics refers to all offensive and defensive 1v1 situations and forms the basis for an understanding of tactical play. It should be an important part of soccer training, particularly in the early years, because all of the more advanced tactical measures build on individual tactics. Legendary coach Wiel Coerver allows a player to advance to group tactics only after he has perfected individual tactics.

In 1v1 play, a player cannot hide and is forced to assume responsibility, which young players must learn early on.

Brazil's star player Neymar—individual tactics at the highest level

9.2   GROUP TACTICS

Group tactics include all planned defensive and offensive actions carried out by two or more players.

An offensive example would be a one-two pass or playing with a third man.

In defense this would be, for instance, shifting the back four.

Example for a group tactical offensive strategy: playing with a third man

9.3   TEAM TACTICS

All of the individual and group tactics are then systematically combined into team tactics.

The terms *formation* and *system of play* are important concepts that are closely linked to team tactics.

Team tactics, a good game concept, as well as a suitable system of play help to counteract soccer's complexity.

In soccer, this is extremely important because, as previously mentioned, no other team sport possesses such a high degree of complexity.

Along with team, group, and individual tactics, it is also necessary to keep track of which team is in possession of the ball.

For this reason, the two concepts
- attacking tactics
> **own team in possession and**
- defensive tactics
> **opposing team in possession**

as well as the **four phases of a soccer game** must always be included in tactical planning and implementation.

CHAPTER 10

The Four Phases
of the Game

CHAPTER 10

The Four Phases
of the Game

"There are people who think that soccer is a matter of life and death. I don't like that mindset. I assure you, it is much more serious than that."

Passionate soccer—for many it is more than a game

To make tactical decisions, a coach must be able to interpret the four phases of the game.

Every soccer game can be divided into the following four phases.

Phase 1:

Own team has possession; opponent is organized.

Phase 2:

Opponent has possession; own team is disorganized.

Phase 3:

Opponent has possession; own team is organized.

Phase 4:

Own team has possession; opponent is disorganized.

Important: The top objective is to be dominant in all four phases of the game, because when this is the case, the chances of victory increase tremendously.

Every coach has to know how the opposing team behaves during these four phases and must find ways for his team to work with that knowledge.

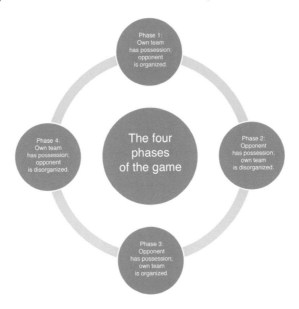

10.1 PHASE 1

OWN TEAM HAS POSSESSION; OPPONENT IS ORGANIZED.

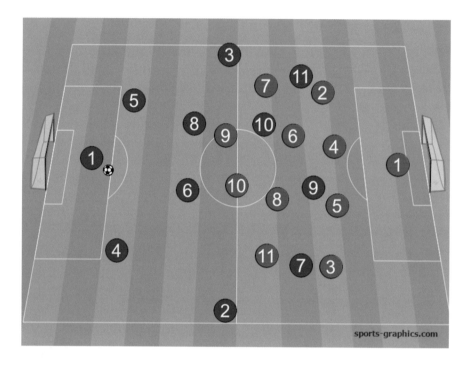

sports-graphics.com

During the first phase, one's own team has possession, and the opponent is organized.

The following items are important for creating chances and scoring goals:

- Fanning out: covering the field in depth and width
- Using short passes: low and accurate balls
- Create passing opportunities:

> **Getting open/signaling availability**

> **Playing without the ball**

> **Forming triangles and diamonds**

> **Opening up passing lanes**

- Switching play quickly
- Changing rhythm of play
- Playing across lines

- Final balls: Centers and long balls
- Rule: Diagonal run   straight pass
       Straight pass   diagonal pass
- Superior number and dangerous situations via successful, offensive 1v1 situations
- Aspire to have the courage to take risks, especially in the forward zone.
- Work with few touches and brief contact times to quickly create combinations in open spaces.

10.2 PHASE 2

OPPONENT HAS POSSESSION; OWN TEAM IS DISORGANIZED.

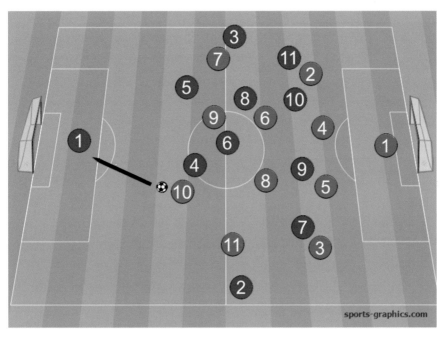

During phase 2, one's own team had possession and lost the ball, because of a bad pass, for example.

The following behavior is important here:

- First question: Is counter-pressing an option here?
- If the answer is no, the team must switch from offense to defense as quickly as possible.

- As many players as possible should be moved behind the ball as quickly as possible.
- The opponent's space must be reduced.
- During equal number situations or when outnumbered, protecting the goal always takes precedence over capturing the ball.
- Narrow the playing areas in a funnel-like formation.

10.3 PHASE 3

OPPONENT HAS POSSESSION; OWN TEAM IS ORGANIZED.

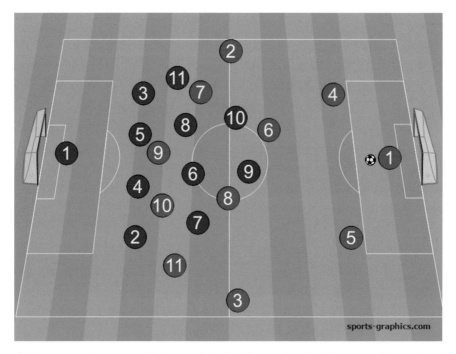

sports-graphics.com

If the opponent was unable to exploit the disorganization, the team has entered phase 3.

The one's own team has reorganized, and the opponent has possession.

Now the goal is to actively win the ball.

- ALL players systematically participate in defense.
- The team forms a compact defensive block with short distances and narrows the spaces using ball-oriented defense in order to establish a superior number situation near the ball.
- Block the passing lanes.
- Create a safe distance from team's own goal.
- Form defensive triangles to create an optimal defensive shadow.
- Reduce playing space.
- Pay attention to staggering for depth.
- Play positive, aggressive 1v1 without fouls.
- Systematically capture the ball using practiced pressing strategies.

10.4 PHASE 4

OWN TEAM'S POSSESSION; OPPONENT IS DISORGANIZED.

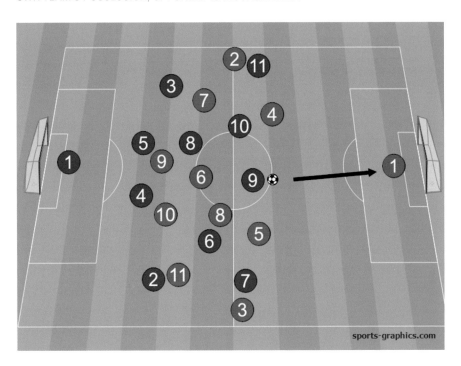

sports-graphics.com

One's own team now captures the ball and plays against a disorganized opponent.

This phase lasts until the opponent has reorganized, which is why it is important to exploit the disorganization and do so as quickly as possible, as the average window of opportunity is 6 to 10 seconds before the opponent's defense has reorganized.

These items is important if the disorganization is to be exploited:

- A counterattack does not inevitably mean that there is a superior number, but in most cases it indicates the opponent's disorganization.
- Quickly switchover from defense to offense.
- Exploit the opponent's disorganization.
- First look forward.
- Pass into the seam area.
- It is critical that the forwards run their paths at top speed or use tempo dribbling toward the goal.
- If a quick counterattack is not possible, the ball should be safeguarded and the game rebuilt, taking the team back to phase 3.

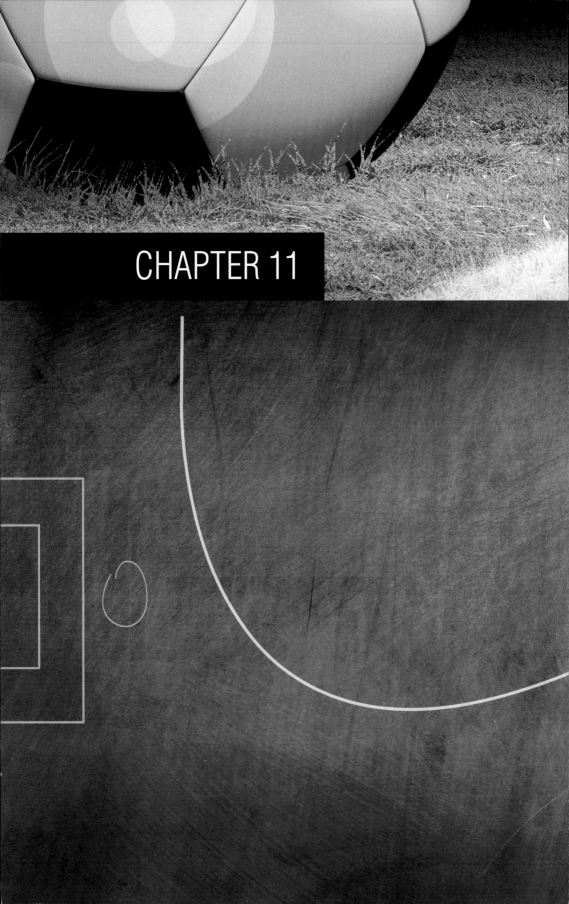

CHAPTER 11

Perfect Switching Play:
The Key to Success

CHAPTER 11

Perfect Switching Play: The Key to Success

"When I was younger, I always tried to do what I thought was right, not what was right for the game."

Henry Thierry (World Champion, European champion, global superstar)

*A*s we already saw in the four phases, the game of soccer is characterized by lots of possession changes between teams; frequently there are multiple changes in possession during just one minute of playing time.

Because of this frequency in possession change, *switching play* is one of soccer's most important principles.

If the switch to defense is too slow, a team can be hit on the counterattack; if the switch to offense is too slow, potential open spaces are already blocked.

The perfect switching play practiced by FC Barcelona in 2008 under coach Pep Guardiola further increased the already growing significance of switching play.

In general, *switching play* in soccer refers to the moment the ball switches from one team to the other.

All of the players have to know precisely how they must respond the moment a turnover takes place.

Switching play can basically be divided into two categories:
*   Switching play when gaining possession
*   Switching play with a turnover

You must practice switching play

11.1 SWITCHING PLAY WHEN GAINING POSSESSION

Roate!

As soon as possession has been taken, the player should immediately look forward in order to quickly take advantage of the opponent's disorganization.

important
timing

Here the benchmark *10-second rule*—the time it takes a player to get reorganized—surfaces again. Top teams generally even try for immediate counter-pressing and only require 6 to 8 seconds of reorganization time.

The goal is to play a long pass into the seams or move into open and dangerous spaces with a fast dribble to quickly score.

11.2 SWITCHING PLAY WITH A TURNOVER

After a turnover the first thing to do is to assess whether a quick counterattack within the first five seconds is an option.

If this is not possible, all players must try to reestablish their defensive formation as quickly as possible in order to narrow the width and depth of the playing space. Then players must use this compactness to work against the ball.

Usually the player closest to the ball immediately puts pressure on the ball to minimize the opponent's ability to continue play.

Ideally the player who is putting pressure on the player in possession of the ball should always be at the front of the defensive triangle so that the opponent's dangerous long balls can be stopped.

In doing so, every player assumes the position closest to where he is at the moment. The object is to avoid unnecessary running paths.

Funnel-like narrowing of the running paths blocks the dangerous center.

Every coach must give his players specific instructions for switching play to ensure quick action during high-speed play.

Key word: Anticipation

Generally what is important when switching play in offense as well as defense is the ability to anticipate playing situations and be prepared in advance for a switch in play.

Here, a *bodyguard* is often put in place through a staggered formation in the midfield to protect the other players. The job of a bodyguard is to close dangerous seams and spaces that can develop in the offense during a turnover.

German national team player Sami Khedira of Real Madrid does a tremendous job with the practical application of this theme.

During defensive actions, such as an opponent's corner, for example, at least one attacking player—or better yet, two or three—should be thinking offensively to optimally exploit a possible counterattack with possession.

If the defense's goalie intercepts the ball after a corner, the attacking players immediately try to break away from the opponent to start into an open space.

The number of players near the ball also plays an important role in well-executed switching play.

Creating superior number situations using extra running effort and good tactical play generates many options for continued play with possession and the opportunity to immediately put pressure on the opposing team and regain possession after a turnover.

When two teams execute their switching play at the same skill level, it is important to read situations before the opponent does and act faster.

These important performance factors, such as game intelligence and quick responses, can be trained with appropriate styles of play during practice. Practice is often performed on small fields on which players are constantly confronted with changing numbers of opponents.

It is important that these types of play always take place in the *original tactical space* in order to simulate real-time competitive play as closely as possible.

Some top teams now use a *countdown clock*. This countdown clock is operated by the coach.

For instance, when a team loses possession during a training match, the countdown clock counts down five seconds. If the ball is recaptured, the clock counts down 10 seconds, which means that the players gradually get used to the timeframe standardized by top international soccer.

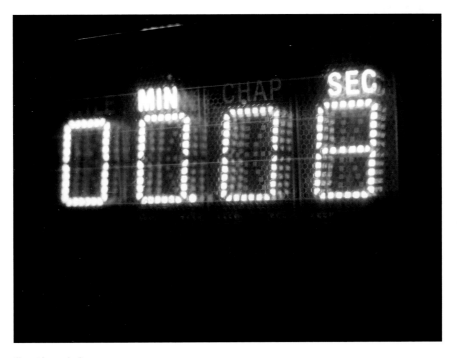

Countdown clock

CHAPTER 12

Zone Play

CHAPTER 12

Zone Play

"Soccer is very simple, but simple soccer is the most difficult."

Soccer legend Johan Cruyff

The Netherland's revolutionary game concept of *totaalvoetbal*—characterized primarily by the 1974 and 1978 World Cups, when the team made it to the final game, and by coach Rinus Michels—resulted in a switch from 1v1 defense to zone defense and to *zone soccer*, the principles of which we will now examine more closely.

Within the context of *totaalvoetbal*, the concept of *positional play*—which presupposes that the positions in a basic formation must always be occupied—is important.

However, which player who will specifically occupy this zone is of secondary importance.

Here, the term zone is more appropriate than *position* because zone already implies a space within which action is flexible and no fixed positions exist.

The principles of zone soccer provide an ideal model for ball-oriented play.

In soccer, the objective of defense is to place more players than the offense close to the ball and to use open zones, or rather to block these open zones as best as possible. (Similarly, the offense tries to place more players than the defense close to the ball.)

When two different systems of play meet up, it is easier to create superior numbers in some spaces and more difficult in others.

Therefore, the key to success in defense is to narrow the space the opponent plays in, and in offense, the goal is to make the space as large as possible.

In modern soccer, all players must participate in the effort to gain possession; here the distance between the back line and the far front line should ideally not exceed 27 to 33 yards so that a compact block can be formed.

This narrows the spaces and puts so much pressure on the opponent that he does not have time to outplay the last line of defense, which has moved way up. The offside rule provides some additional help here.

In this model, your team simultaneously decreases the running paths because the space in which the opponent is attacked has to be kept as small as possible.

12.1 LATERAL AXIS

First, the field is divided into five zones along the lateral axis.

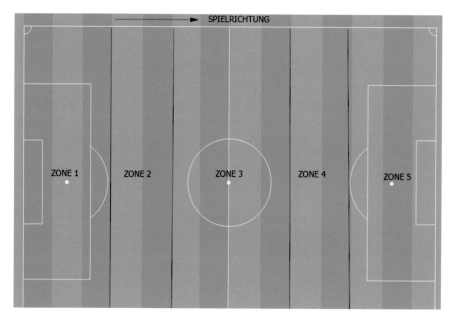

Zone 1: Goal safety zone

Zone 2: Defense zone

Zone 3: Midfield zone

Zone 4: Attacking zone

Zone 5: Forechecking zone

Please note: The individual zones vary depending on the game situation. They can even merge. The risk level increases with each advancing zone in the direction of play because the distance to one's own goal increases.

12.2 LONGITUDINAL AXIS

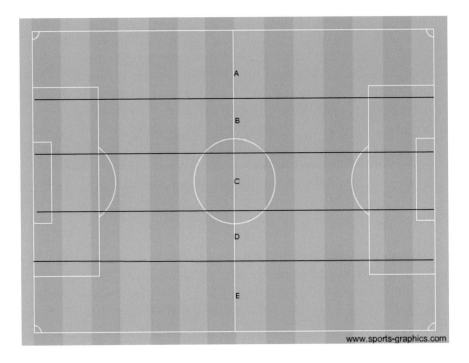

www.sports-graphics.com

The longitudinal axis is also divided into five zones, whereby A and E delineate the zones for the outside lanes, B and D the halfway zones, and C the middle zone.

12.3 LONGITUDINAL AND LATERAL AXES

The longitudinal and lateral axes are laid on top of each other, creating 25 different zones.

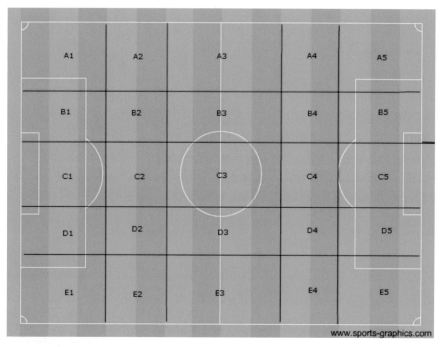

As can be seen here, zone C3 is larger than the other zones, which is why many coaches seek to control the middle zone. But the result of focusing on the middle zone is that zones A and E could possibly have open spaces.

12.4 CONCLUSIONS

The following conclusions can be drawn from using zone defense:

- The aim is always to place more defensive players than offensive players close to the ball in the zone created by the longitudinal and lateral axes.

- In doing so, the middle axis (zones C, B, D) must always be covered because the goal is in the middle zone, and opportunities for continued play happen most often here.

- The outside lane must always be covered when an opponent gains possession there.

- The lane away from the ball remains open. However, at the highest level of play, the off-ball defender no longer comes in as far as was common a few years ago. Maintaining a little more distance allows him quicker access to the often very strong dribblers in the outside lanes with a wide diagonal ball.

- During play, defense players try to keep the distances to the opponents as small as possible so that their actions can be compact, and they can try to regain possession with skillful defensive strategies.

- During offense play, coverage of the field must be optimal; there must be as much breadth and depth as possible to counteract defense tactics.

- It has been observed for some time that top teams during offensive action often move their two outside lane players to the center to create superior numbers in a somewhat larger space than the frequently used "double-18-yard area."

A remarkable number of goals originate from this corridor that is referred to by some coaches as the *danger zone*.

Often the decisive pass is played from the danger zone, or a counterattack begins in this zone after a bad pass, which is why the two outside midfielders consciously move to the center to create a superior number situation there.

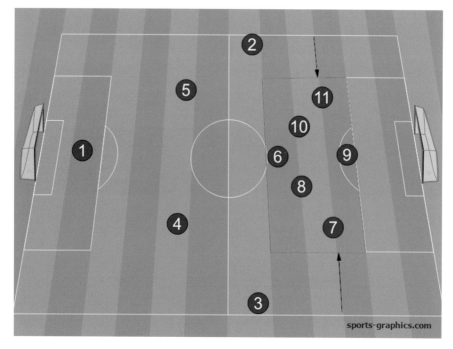

sports-graphics.com

Creating a superior number in the danger zone by moving outside lane players to the center

Another option for creating a superior number in the middle of the field during offense is to shift the off-ball wingback from the back four to the defensive midfield position. This option is particularly effective against teams that work with only one striker.

Whenever the on-ball wingback moves to the ball, the off-ball central defender usually moves up, and the on-ball central defender follows.

But rather than moving the off-ball wingback laterally, usually a better variation against one striker is to move the off-ball wingback to the defensive midfield position, thereby creating forward pressure and placing a superior number in the middle of the field. This variation will also have a positive effect during counter-pressing in the case of a turnover.

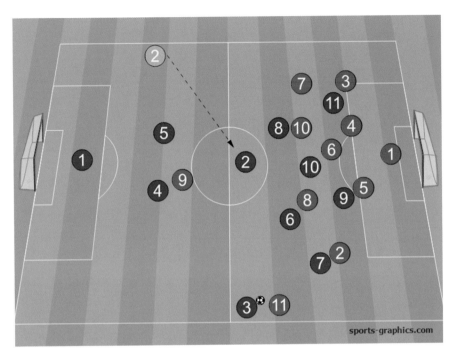

Building forward pressure by moving the off-ball wingback to the defensive midfield position

CHAPTER 13

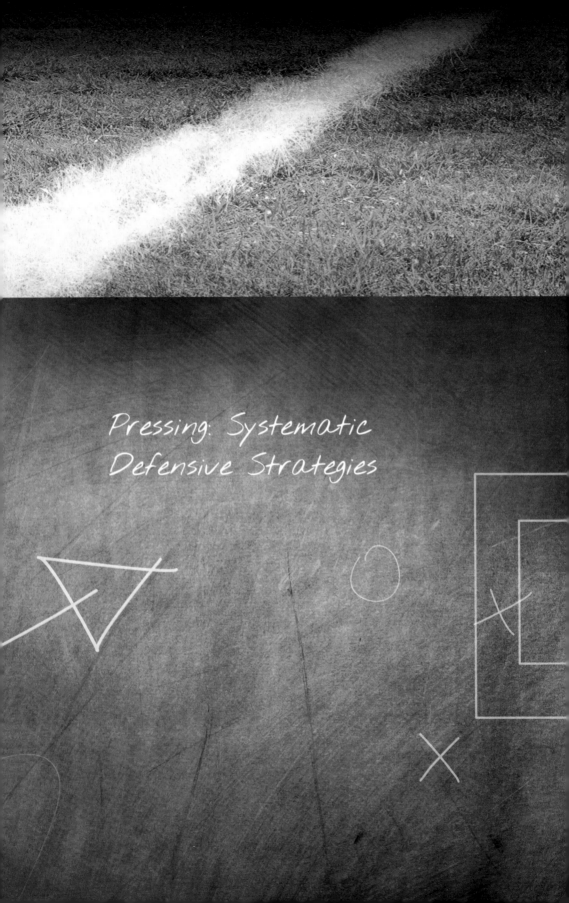

Pressing: Systematic Defensive Strategies

CHAPTER 13

Pressing: Systematic Defensive Strategies

"Any chain is only as strong as its weakest link, and the whole is always greater than the sum of its parts!"

As the zone soccer model shows, defensive strategies play a very important role in soccer. The basis for this is pressing, which should be a very important component of every match.

Russian player and coach, Victor Maslov—who scored many victories with this innovation, particularly during the 1960s—is considered the originator of pressing in soccer.

Cunning coach Victor Maslov

Great coaches such as Rinus Michels, Walerij Lobanowskyj, Arrigo Sacchi, and Pep Guardiola continued to advance and refine different pressing strategies.

Pressing is the planned attempt to disrupt the opposing team early on, to create superior number situations, to force errors, and to prevent a possible pass to a teammate close to the ball by blocking spaces and closely marking players, or at least forcing a wide pass.

So the purpose of pressing in soccer is to control the opposing team using planned strategic behavior in order to gain possession of the ball. A high degree of compactness within the individual sections of the team is critical for the success of a pressing action.

Pressing play means to gain possession collectively. In other words, the entire team must participate.

Pressing play allows the players to protect each other and create superior number situations near the ball.

Important principles

- Offensive players must also perform defensive actions.
- The system of the one's own team as well as the opponent's must be taken into account.
- Where does defensive play take place?
- How do I gain possession?
- What does the opponent's build-up look like?
- Must understand the basic order and formation of the one's own team and the opponent's.

Furthermore, all participants must understand what might trigger a pressing.

The following are possible triggers:

- "Pressing victim"
- A pass into a specific zone
- Technical errors
- Opponent is not open in playing direction
- Goal deficit
- Situational, as with a throw-in, for example

It is also important that every player knows where and how pressing should occur.

We differentiate four types of pressing

- defensive pressing,
- midfield pressing,
- offensive pressing, and
- counter-pressing.

We will now elaborate on these four types.

13.1 DEFENSIVE PRESSING

Defensive pressing is the most defensive and, at the same time, most passive pressing variation.

The aim is to form a compact and closed unit behind the ball and wait for the opponent.

Here, it is almost impossible to act deliberately and control the opponent, which is why defensive pressing should only be used on a situation-by-situation basis.

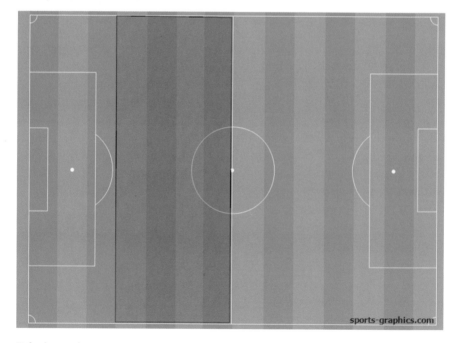

Defensive pressing zone

In doing so, the back four defend close to their own 18-yard area and wait until the ball reaches their own half.

Defensive pressing is often either imposed by a dominant opponent or used to run down the clock with a slim lead.

The advantage of defensive pressing is the extremely compact team unit that is not susceptible to allowing balls to pass behind the defensive line.

In addition, when gaining possession of the ball, large spaces open up in forward play.

The disadvantage is that defensive pressing is purely reactive instead of proactive because protecting the goal is the main objective.

Moreover, a turnover causes wide open spaces in the basic formation.

Furthermore, the strikers have to cover long distances to the opposing goal, and the opponent can play balls into the danger zone.

Additionally, it becomes difficult to withstand the constant pressure generated by the opponent with high balls into the center of defense.

13.2 MIDFIELD PRESSING

Midfield pressing is the most often used form of pressing and takes place approximately 16 to 22 yards into one's own half or 16 to 22 yards into the opposing half.

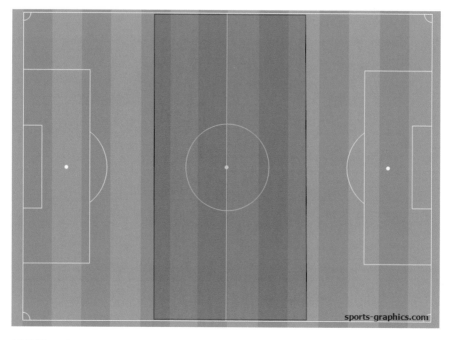

sports-graphics.com

Midfield pressing zone

The opponent is initially permitted to initiate play.

At the same time, attempts are made to direct the ball toward specific opposing players into specific spaces.

These are then purposefully attacked, and the surrounding passing options are blocked.

The strikers wait for the opponent approximately 16 to 22 yards in front of the halfway line.

The defensive line is positioned approximately 33 yards in front of the defense's goal.

As soon as the opposing team plays into the midfield pressing zone, the players attempt to create a superior number situation near the ball.

Some coaches even refer to a "battle zone" where players should stand close to the opponents and defend aggressively.

With all pressing strategies, it is important that the distances between individual team sections are very short.

Midfield pressing offers three major advantages in particular:

- If the opponent should manage to extricate himself from the press, the defensive line is still able to protect.
- It is not too far away from the defender's goal, which allows for good teamwork with the goalie to prevent possible long balls.
- The distance to the opposing goal is short, which is the ideal condition for a quick counterattack.

13.3 OFFENSIVE PRESSING

Offensive pressing is the most offensive form of the defensive strategies presented here.

The zone in which offensive pressing is played extends from the halfway line to the opposing back line.

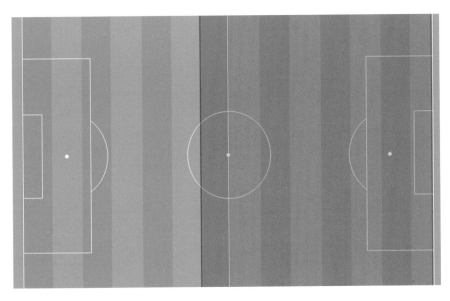

Offensive zone

All players move up far enough to completely block the opponent in his own half.

Because of the high intensity, offensive pressing can only be played in phases such as, for instance, at the start of the game to catch the opponent off guard, after the halftime break, or in case of a goal deficit just before the end of the game. But this type of pressing is also popular on a situational basis, such as with a goal kick or a throw-in.

A classic example of extremely offensive pressing is the team Red Bull Salzburg coached by Roger Schmidt during the 2013/2014 season.

The Dutch record-holding champions Ajax Amsterdam were clearly defeated twice due to extreme pressing in the European League.

FC Bayern Munich also suffered a 0-3 loss in a tryout match against Red Bull Salzburg.

Offense is often the best defense, particularly against a better team.

Roger Schmidt

Roger Schmidt's comment: "Passivity is not the answer against Bayern Munich."

Salzburg defends with an extremely running-intensive and highly concentrated style of play, most often from a 1-4-4-2 formation, so far up field that the opponent's center defense is immediately put under pressure after a short pass. Salzburg then defends forward until either they gain possession of the ball or it has to be cleared with a long uncontrolled ball.

A clearly visible trend when identifying young soccer talent is the increasing attention on players who possess the skills and the passion for extremely offensive pressing and want to defend forward.

The difference to midfield pressing is often quite fluid as offensive pressing often originates from midfield pressing.

The players' starting position is the same as midfield pressing.

Important: If forward movement is too fast, there is a major risk that the opponent will immediately play a long ball; the opponent should, therefore, initially be given an opening and then be steered into advantageous situations using practiced patterns.

A situational offensive pressing is an exception where, for instance, a goal kick is conceded in order to provoke a desired long ball. This type of offensive pressing is often used against strong teams.

In the final offensive pressing position, all players have pushed forward into the opposing half.

The opposing team is controlled in its own half through aggressive forechecking.

Efforts are made to actively defend forward in order to take away the opponent's time and space to safely build up their play.

Pressure on the opponent must be so strong that it causes errors.

The problem is that one's own team is also under pressure and unable to recover.

The extreme shifting ensures that when gaining possession, hardly a player is in position.

Loss of focus is often punished with long balls behind the back four where large spaces open up, resulting in the immediate threat of a goal.

Here the goalie's participation is of particular importance.

A successful antidote for evading offensive pressing is long, diagonal balls behind the back four, quick shifts in play, as well as playing across lines.

Another remedy that is seen with increasing frequency in top teams is the *anti-pressing ball*. Here the opponent's offensive pressing is anticipated early.

After the central defender passes to the wingback, the opposing attacker blocks the option of a return pass to the central defender.

Now the wingback plays over the blocked central defender with a wide pass to the central defender away from the ball to counter the opponent's shifting. The offense can then conveniently continue play to the wingback or the outside midfield player.

Anti-pressing ball

13.4 COUNTER-PRESSING

"Counter-pressing is my go-to play."

(Jürgen Klopp)

Counter-pressing is the immediate collective action against the ball after a turnover to regain possession as quickly as possible.

In contrast to defensive, midfield, and offensive pressing, here the action against the ball does not take place with the defensive system but rather starts immediately after a turnover.

Ideally, counter-pressing happens within five seconds while the opposing team has not yet perfectly adjusted to possession play. Consequently, the likelihood of scoring a goal increases.

Strictly speaking, the term *counter-pressing* is not quite correct since the term implies that there has been a previous pressing, which statistics show happens very rarely.

Analyses show that while counter-pressing requires a lot of energy in the short-term, it does conserve energy in the long-term because the amount of energy required to regain possession when the opposing team lets the ball circulate and shifts play is considerably higher

In particular, FC Barcelona's successes in recent years, in which counter-pressing played a pivotal role, inspired many coaches to employ this defensive strategy.

Important here is the team's starting position prior to a turnover, which is why top teams that employ this strategy constantly try to create superior number situations near the ball.

On the one hand, this is an offensive advantage, but on the other hand, it is an important aspect of immediate counter-pressing.

No matter how quickly a team can switch gears after a turnover and aggressively move forward against the ball, counter-pressing is only successful if prior positioning of the individual players is optimal.

Another important aspect is the intelligence of the players who first recognize the pressing signals, interpret them correctly, and, finally, act correctly.

Important aspects of counter-pressing:

- Readiness of all players to participate in counter-pressing.
- The player on the ball must be attacked ideally from all sides.
- Ball-oriented shifting by the defensive midfield.
- The back four also shift slightly to the front to stay connected.
- Depending on the play, the wingback near the ball often shifts far to the front.
- Brain work: Players must react with lightning speed after a turnover and immediately work against the ball because otherwise the opportunity for counter-pressing is not used.
- Approximately five-second windows of opportunity: If the ball cannot be recaptured during this timeframe, a compact defensive formation must be established as quickly as possible.

CHAPTER 14

Formations
and Systems of Play

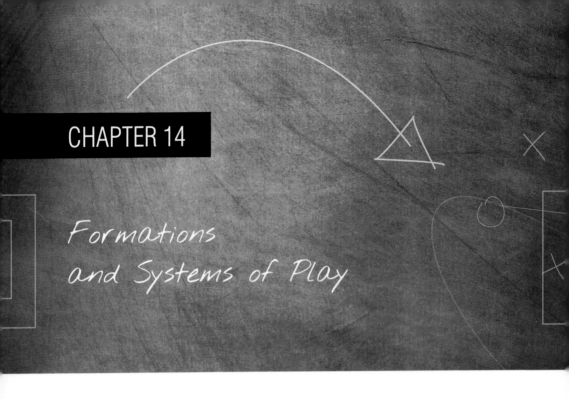

CHAPTER 14

Formations and Systems of Play

"Anyone who wants to win needs a system."

Star coach José Mourinho gives tactical instructions during training.

*T*he difference between the two terms *formation* and *system of play* is of fundamental importance.

A *basic formation* is the lineup and shows the manning of positions during possession in offense as well as during play against the ball in defense.

A *system of play* is then formed from the basic formation and has different characteristics, depending on whether the team has possession or works against the ball.

The system of play brings the basic formation to life.

The behaviors of different positions are derived from the game concept, tactical ideas, and the formation, which ideally will bear the coach's hallmarks in a system of play on the field.

Thus, the system of play offers information about the interpretation and behavior of the different positions. For example, does the wingback get involved in offensive play, or does he stay in his position?

These formations, such as 1-4-4-2 or 1-3-5-2, are represented by a combination of numbers.

The first digit always represents the goalie, the second digit the number of defensive players, the third digit the number of midfielders, and the fourth the number of attacking players.

Very important here is the coach's ability to optimally position the players on the field—which also depends on the opponent—to create superior number situations and equalize inferior number situations, which is done by means of the systems of play.

What matters is that these formations are never viewed as permanent structures.

These permanent structures only exist on paper or at the kick-off.

CLARIFICATION BY EXAMPLE

Basic formation: 1-4-3-3

The basic formation 1-4-3-3 at the start of the game can quickly change during possession to 1-2-3-2-3 and to 1-4-2-3-1 during defense, depending on the situation. Consequently, players must be tactically well trained and flexible.

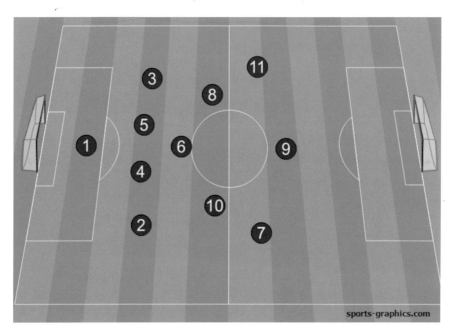

Basic formation of 1-4-3-3

The 1-4-3-3
Can morph into @
4-2-3-1 defensively.

SYSTEM OF PLAY AGAINST THE BALL: 1-4-2-3-1

The variable behavior on the individual positions in this formation results in a 1-4-2-3-1 system of play during defensive play with shifting against the ball.

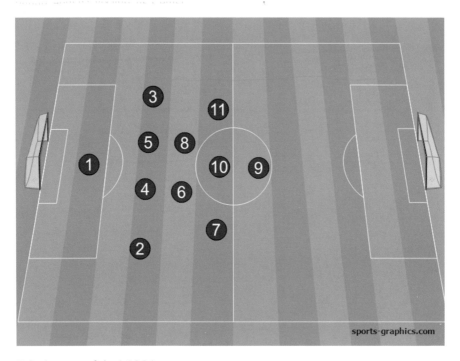

Defensive system of play 1-4-2-3-1

Teams that play from a basic 1-4-3-3 formation often switch to a 1-4-2-3-1 during defensive play, ensuring good compactness because the two defensive midfielders provide additional support to the center. Positions 11 and 7 drop back one line and form a three-point line with 10.

Position 8 moves back and forms a "double six" with 6.

Position 9 tries to control the center back.

SYSTEM OF PLAY WITH POSSESSION: 1-2-3-2-3

When the team gets possession, the two wingbacks are now positioned wide and shift up. Position 6 drops back, and 8 moves up correspondingly.

Positions 11 and 7 also shift up but are not on the same line as 2 and 3. If they were, opportunities for continued play would be blocked.

This results in a 1-2-3-2-3 formation with possession during offensive play.

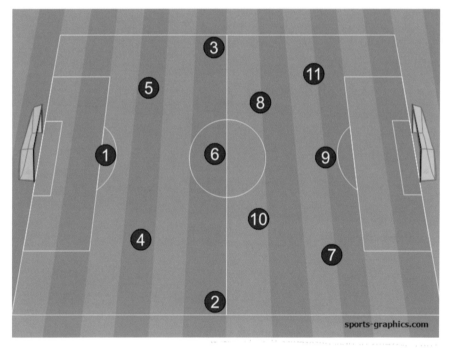

Offensive system of play: 1-2-3-2-3

Nearly all top teams are flexible in their actions. It is ideal for the team to vary the system with possession, particularly during offensive play. This formation variation keeps the opponent from adjusting because one's own team is difficult to figure out.

With a basic 1-4-3-3 formation, it would make sense to practice the 1-3-3-4 with possession as an additional more offensive variation to the 1-2-3-2-3, especially when trying to use the advantages of the *dynamic back three* and exert lots of pressure. This can be done very well with this system during possession with the four players in the front line completely neutralizing the opponent's back four.

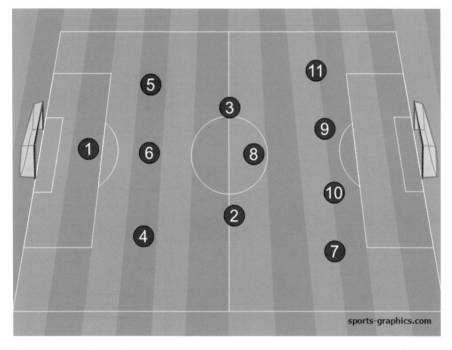

Offensive system of play: 1-3-3-4

Thus, systems of play determine the players' respective positions and spaces.

However, a system of play does not convey the strategy!

Formations and systems of play are only brought to life by strategic instructions...

The system only conveys the players' tasks, whereby these must also be accurately defined by the coach because the same playing position can and will be interpreted differently within a system of play.

The exception here is the goalie whose job is nearly always the same, regardless of the basic formation and system of play. Because the goalie's role remains the same, teams have gotten into the habit of not taking into account the goalie when designating the numeric formation.

In this book, the goalie is mentioned explicitly within the context of formations and systems of play as this emphasizes the great importance of the goalie, especially to adolescents.

The goalie is not called goalkeeper, because in modern soccer, his job extends far beyond simply keeping the goal.

Manuel Neuer: Outstanding not only with his hands, but also his feet

"There is more than one truth in soccer."

The past shows us that no one system is necessarily better than another.

Every system has advantages and disadvantages. What matters is the coach's ability to ensure balance on the playing field, to create superior number situations, and to prevent inferior ones, as well as the skill of the players who must optimally implement this system.

To date, big tournaments in soccer have been won in completely different ways and with completely different game concepts, formations, and systems of play.

In soccer, every system of play is justified, and while it does not have to be popular, it must be accepted.

But it is implausible for a team to practice strictly offensive soccer during the week, then limit itself defensively to counterattacking in a 1-5-3-2 formation and playing long balls.

Because of the frequently changing playing situations, the many positional changes, and a high degree of creativity during possession, it is easier to practice behaviors during systems of play in defense rather than offense, which is why most coaches start out working on defense when taking over a new team.

In addition, a coach must be aware that a system of play always has fitness-related implications.

Depending on which systems of play encounter each other, it can result in a considerably greater running effort in order to equalize inferior number situations or use open spaces, for example.

Thus, comments like "I felt as though the opponent played with one extra player" are not unusual in soccer.

14.1   GAME-ORIENTED OR SYSTEM-ORIENTED

"The football of the past we have to respect, the football of today we must study, and the game of the future we should anticipate."

Bora Milutinović (five-time World Cup participant)

A coach generally has two options to determine a system of play:

A) GAME-ORIENTED

The coach depends on the playing resources available to him on which to then build a system of play.

Or

B) SYSTEM-ORIENTED

The coach chooses a preferred system of play in advance and assembles his squad based on his system, which, however, is the more difficult variation and is extremely complicated, especially in the area of youth and amateur soccer.

With all the importance of tactics in soccer, it should be clear that in the end it is not the system that will determine victory or defeat but rather the quality of the individual players and their ability to put the chosen system into practice.

It is the coach's job to absolutely understand the advantages and disadvantages of a system of play so he can find the best possible system for his players.

In addition, this knowledge will allow him to react to the opponent's system and make adjustments.

But if all teams were to choose the same system of play like that of Bayern Munich or the Spanish national team, for instance, soccer would be only half as exciting because these teams most often have the best individual players and therefore would always win.

Nevertheless, there are always teams that make life difficult for these top teams.

Take, for instance, the national team of the Faroe Islands, which have roughly 50,000 inhabitants and whose team, which is still manned with recreational players, makes life difficult for opponents due to improvements in the area of tactics and athletics. This is something that national teams with highly paid pros, such as Portugal or Austria, have learned the hard way.

One thing is for certain:

Good organization can, to some extent, balance deficiencies in the individual quality of players, which brings a lot of excitement to the game of soccer and contributes to a David beating a Goliath.

14.2 THE THREE BASIC FORMATIONS

Based on soccer history, there are essentially only three *basic formations* that all other formations and systems of play build on:

A) 1-4-4-2

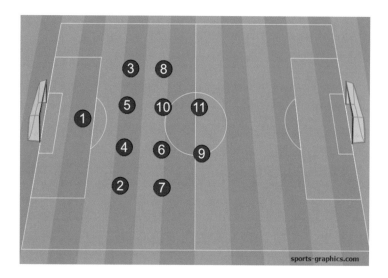

B) 1-4-3-3

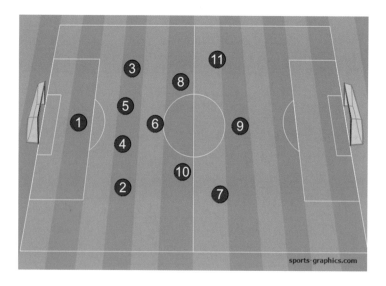

C) 1-5-3-2

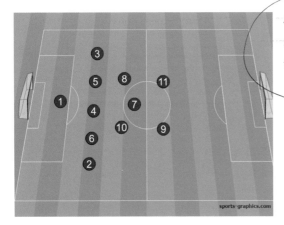

All other basic formations in soccer were and are derived from these basic formations.

14.3 COMMON SYSTEMS OF PLAY IN MODERN SOCCER

Below is a detailed explanation of the current most popular systems of play, based on the three basic formations, with their strengths and weaknesses. It must be noted that today nearly all top teams use different formations for defensive and offensive play in order to optimally use the advantages of individual systems.

1-4-4-2:

> 1-4-4-2 line

> 1-4-4-2 diamond

1-4-3-3

> 1-4-2-3-1

> 1-4-1-4-1

Systems of play with three-man lines

> 1-5-3-2

> 1-3-5-2

> 1-3-4-3

use one formation for attacking and a different one for defending

A) 1-4-4-2 LINE

The basis for all modern systems of play is the 1-4-4-2 in a line.

Originally devised by Victor Maslov, the 1-4-4-2 caught on in reaction to the dominant 1-4-4-3-formation of the 1970s and 1980s.

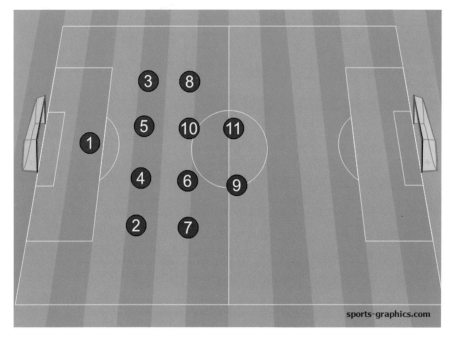

1-4-4-2 in a line

The tasks within a ball-oriented game are particularly apparent in this system.

Once the position-specific tasks in this system are mastered, the switch to other systems is often significantly easier.

The 1-4-4-2 in a line is very popular with many coaches because it is very adaptable from a tactical standpoint and can be interpreted offensively as well as defensively.

The space can be optimally configured, and with the 1-4-4-2, the width of the playing field is well covered.

In offensive play, wing play combinations are made possible by doubling up in the outside lanes.

The two lines of four form a compact team unit that is narrowed with a consistent allocation of the spaces, resulting in a close link between the sections of the team.

With a midfield of four in a line, a good formation is most often the focus during play against the ball.

A doubling up in the center allows the opponent little room for combination play near the goal.

The wings are always manned without the wingbacks having to move up too far. However, this leaves a significantly larger gap between the strikers and the center midfield.

This system lacks an open man in the center, which is why creativity has to come from the wings.

ADVANTAGES AND DISADVANTAGES OF THE 1-4-4-2 LINE

Advantages
- Optimal spatial allocation and high compatibility. This results in an economical running effort.
- Creation of superior number situations is very feasible.
- Good protection in the midfield center with two midfielders.
- Good opportunities in wing play with the doubling of the wing.
- The coach has many opportunities for tactical interpretations.

Disadvantages
- Lines can be overplayed with long, vertical passes.
- Fewer opportunities on offense for triangulation than other systems.
- More difficult to switch play on defense, especially when the two wingbacks have moved up a ways.

- Possibly insufficient creativity due to the lack of a typical playmaker.
- The two strikers often have to fend for themselves.

B) 1-4-4-2 DIAMOND

The 1-4-4-2 with a diamond offers lots of advantages for a team that wants to play offensively.

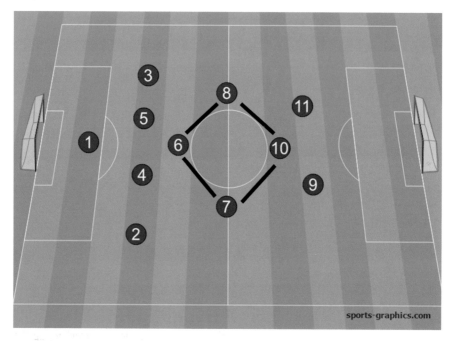

1-4-4-2 diamond

The diamond in a 1-4-4-2 formation can be interpreted very offensively, particularly with widely spaced and far forward wingbacks.

The former Bayern Munich coach and current national team coach for the Netherlands, Louis van Gaal, is one of the proponents of this formation; but other teams such as Borussia Dortmund under Jürgen Klopp have also benefited from the advantages of the diamond.

That is to say, it is easy to form triangles and, as the name suggests, diamonds.

When working in a diamond, most often there is a superior number in the center because there are four players where the opponent usually has positioned only two or three players.

Because the two outside midfielders have moved to the center, the wingbacks come from a deep position and are able to actively participate in offensive play.

When choosing this system, it is important to also have good wingbacks who are able to optimally fill this space at the side and use the required skills to interpret accordingly.

In contrast to the 1-4-4-2 line, in the diamond, the two strikers are spaced farther apart. This gives the playmaker more space to express his creativity and joy of playing.

But the diamond doesn't make much sense if no typical playmaker is available, which shows the importance of the individual players needed for a system of play.

Because of the high offensive strike count, superior number situations are created in front of the opposing line, which is why this system also works well with a turnover in the center to immediately start counter-pressing with the superior number.

Namely the two strikers and three offensive midfielders provide five offensive players who are able to put lots of pressure on the opposing defense.

When playing in the diamond, it makes it difficult for the opponent to pick the direct path through the middle to the goal. This then forces the option of attacking up the wings.

The diamond often experiences problems down the wings, particularly against opponents who play with a 1-4-3-3 or double wings, because in a diamond, the wings always have inferior numbers.

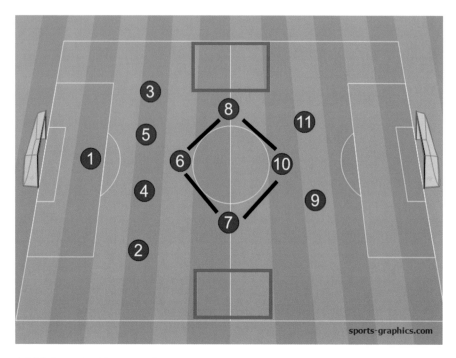

1-4-4-2 diamond problem area—wings

In addition, the wings are often manned by very offensively-thinking wingbacks, which is good during offensive play but extremely problematic with a turnover.

That is where large spaces then open up behind the wingbacks that cannot be closed by the central midfielder or by the two central defenders.

A diamond is, therefore, very vulnerable to counterattacks.

In contrast, the major advantage of the line is that with a turnover, the team can quickly reorganize behind the ball and isn't nearly as vulnerable as with the diamond.

This is why nearly all of the top teams that have chosen a 1-4-4-2 formation combine the defensive advantages of the 1-4-4-2 in a line with the offensive advantages of the diamond formation.

ADVANTAGES AND DISADVANTAGES OF THE 1-4-4-2-DIAMOND

- Advantages
- Emphasis on offensive strengths.
- Superior numbers in the center.
- A typical playmaker shows to advantage.
- Lots of room for the wingbacks in offense with a narrow diamond.
- A diamond is good for starting counter-pressing.

DISADVANTAGES

- Increased vulnerability on the wings.
- Only a center midfielder for protection.
- Increased running effort, especially for wingbacks.
- Very difficult to double the wings due to unmanned wings.
- Major dependence on the types of players needed for this system of play.

C) 1-4-3-3

The 1-4-3-3-formation is closely linked to the name Rinus Michels and the successes of Ajax Amsterdam and FC Barcelona.

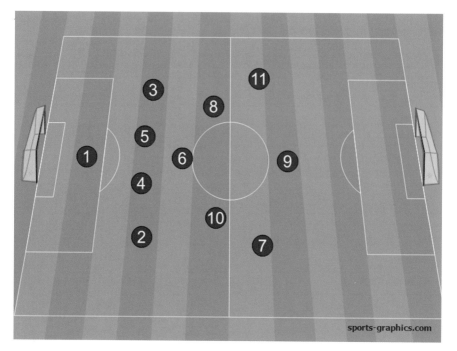

1-4-3-3

In the 1-4-3-3-formation, the width and depth of the field are well covered.

Here long and deep passes can easily cross lines, creating many advantageous 1v1 situations. Players who have been trained specifically for this offensive system can take advantage of these situations.

When a team with a 1-4-3-3-formation positions two defensive and one offensive midfielder in the midfield, it is only a slight variation to a 1-4-2-3-1. This is why the classic 1-4-3-3 is assumed to be an offensive team that wants to dominate by possession and in the 1-4-3-3 plays with a central midfielder behind two offensive midfielders.

The 1-4-3-3 inevitably requires a bold attack and aggressive press in the opponent's half.

With the exception of the now infrequently used 1-4-2-2 employed by Brazil with Pelé in their 1958 world cup victory, it is difficult to play more offensively because there are three nominal strikers on paper.

The system is particularly well suited for when there are bold wing players with strong offensive skills available.

The individual demands of this system on each player are very high which, in professional soccer, also carries with it a financial burden, because this system requires absolutely exceptional players particularly on the wings, who come with a high price tag.

With possession, both midfielders push forward from the halfback positions; however, the corridor along the sideline remains open for the wingbacks.

The center forward's scope of action is in the middle. His movements are usually vertical, when he goes deep and then comes back toward the ball carrier as an open man, for instance.

Another advantage the 1-4-3-3 has in the build-up is an additional opportunity for continued play for the two central defenders who can nearly always deliver a long diagonal ball to the outside lanes that are always manned.

In this system, it is important for the strikers to participate in the effort of gaining possession, which is rarely the case for of a typical wing player because their main focus is offensive play.

One of the two wing players usually participates in build-up play to equalize the nominal inferior number in the midfield.

During defensive play, the two outside offensive wing players can often be seen pulling back somewhat, thereby creating a situational 1-4-2-3-1.

A weak spot in this offensive system of play is that only five field players are thinking about defense.

Next to the back four, the central midfielder is the only anchor for defensive safeguarding, which is why the two halfbacks must be very flexible in their actions.

Often inferior number situations occur when the halfback positions don't work hard enough.

Generally with a turnover during forward movement, the team is automatically outnumbered for a short period of time because only three midfielders are on hand to prevent the counterattack.

ADVANTAGES AND DISADVANTAGES OF THE 1-4-3-3

Advantages

- Well-suited for combination play because of the symmetrical arrangement of the players on the field.
- Facilitates good wing play.
- Very offensive and therefore optimal for action instead of reaction.
- More strikers are trained here than in other systems.
- Very high appeal for spectators.

Disadvantages

- High demands on the individual.
- Inferior number in the midfield.
- Only five defense-oriented players.
- Susceptible to counterattacks.
- Hardly workable without the right types of players on the outside lanes; in addition these types of players are extremely expensive.

D) 1-4-2-3-1

The 1-4-2-3-1-formation is currently one of the most popular systems of play in European elite soccer.

During the 2010 World Cup, three of the four semi-finalists played with this system. Spain used various systems during its 2012 European Championships victory but mainly used the 1-4-2-3-1.

The 1-4-2-3-1 consists of the back four, the double six, an offensive line of three in front of the double six, and a center forward.

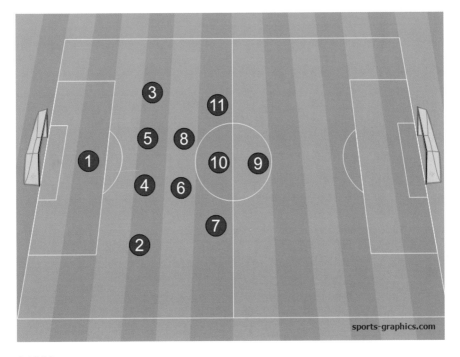

1-4-2-3-1

The major advantage of this system is that it is possible to act nearly anytime from a protected formation.

The center in front of the defensive line is very compact due to the double six.

The outside lanes can quickly be blocked.

At least one defensive midfielder is always on hand for safety during offensive actions, and the wing players can thin out the opposing defense.

A very important factor in this system of play is the double six, which acts as a stabilizing element.

The job of the double six together with the central defenders is to keep the center as compact as possible and to get as much possession as possible in order to subsequently initiate the next attack using strategically skilled actions or possibly to calm down the game.

Anyone who has had a 10v6 practice game with a back four and a double six knows how difficult it is to score goals, even with this superior number.

 When a coach puts a 1-4-2-3-1 on paper, it emphasizes a team's defensive focus because an offensive interpretation would offer a 1-4-3-3.

In a game with a 1-4-2-3-1 formation, the coach should take into account that the outside midfielders have to perform major running efforts, and the wing players need to be very good at 1v1 play.

If the coach decides not to push the central defenders through when the opponent has possession on the wing, the demands on the wing players go up even more.

Another positive aspect to this system is that even typical wing players are able to find a place in the offensive midfield, which is difficult for them in a 1-4-4-2 because there the outside lane must often be interpreted differently.

Of course, compared to the more offensive 1-4-3-3, they must put in more defensive effort, albeit they are able to fully employ their offensive skills during forward movement.

The system also offers many possible ways of controlling the rhythm of play and of varying play on the individual positions.

Depending on the action, it is possible to not only push the wing players up but also to pull them back, or even to move the playmaker higher up to make up a possible deficit.

During defense, the line of three often pulls back very deep, behind the center line, in order to form a compact block with the back four and double six.

 Most often, the single forward blocks the off-ball central defender during the opponent's build-up so that the central defender in possession can only play forward into the compact space.

The opponent frequently tries to get behind the back four with long balls, which is why it is important for the defenders to anticipate and recognize the long balls early and break away and for the goalie to stay vigilant.

ADVANTAGES AND DISADVANTAGES OF THE 1-4-2-3-1

Advantages

- Lots of tactical flexibility.
- Good balance between versatile offensive play and great compactness in defense.
- In its defensive interpretation, it is well suited to counterattacking teams.
- High degree of compactness in the center.

Disadvantages

- Major running effort for players on the outside lanes.
- Open spaces on outside lanes.
- Initial passes from opposing central defenders are difficult to prevent because one forward has a much smaller cover shadow than two forwards.
- Only one striker on offense.

E) 1-4-1-4-1

Many coaches consider the 1-4-1-4-1 a progression of the 1-4-2-3-1, and it is very well suited to teams whose strengths lie in possession play.

But defensive interpretations of this system are also effective, which is why underdogs often resort to this formation.

This system is often successful particularly against a 1-4-4-2 diamond because the outside lanes are strong, and the center has additional support from a center player who works between the lines.

This system became well known through the offensive playing style of Spain and Russia during the 2008 European championships.

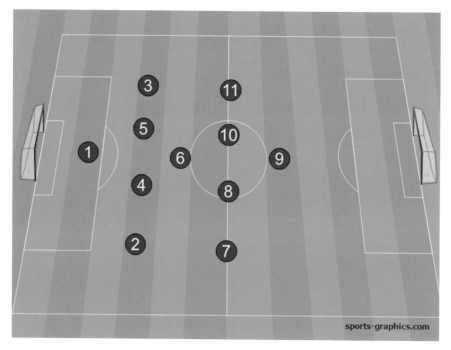

1-4-1-4-1

The advantages of the 1-4-1-4-1 are in the highly compact area of the midfield, the defense, and the option of playing fast combination soccer.

Because of the four vertical and horizontal lines, much of the field's playing area is covered.

The four horizontal lines, in particular, create advantages when trying to win the second ball, as well as many passing opportunities after gaining possession.

Good staggering of players across the width of the field—which can be easily done with two lines of four—allows for quick access to the on-ball player anywhere on the field.

When using this system, long balls played between the central midfielder and the back four are dangerous, because the central midfield has to fend for himself.

In the 1-4-1-4-1, the central midfielder is given a special role.

His job is to keep the opponent from making passes between the lines and to make sure that the back four's actions are compact and solid for as long as possible to prevent the need for the central defenders come forward.

The wings and the center have double the players, and the central midfielder between the lines provides additional support.

This compact staggering in the midfield is designed to limit the opponent's maneuvering space.

In addition, the defensive central midfielder prevents one of the two central defenders from having to move up, which keeps the center compact.

With this system, it is also easy to shift in both directions.

With their team has possession, the wingbacks orient themselves to the outside and push up. From there, they get involved in the attacking play.

The midfield line of four positioned in front of the wingbacks organizes some flexible attacking play.

In doing so, the four midfielders are very offensively oriented. Corresponding positional changes provide lots of attacking flexibility that is difficult for the opponent to figure out.

ADVANTAGES AND DISADVANTAGES OF THE 1-4-1-4-1

Advantages

- Good space allocation and compactness.
- Good variability in attacking play.
- Well suited for combination soccer.
- Double wings.
- Good possibility of winning the second ball.

Disadvantages

- Limited forward play with only one nominal forward.
- Major running effort.
- Only one central defender for safety.
- Danger with balls between the lines of four.
- High tactical demands.

F) 1-5-3-2

The more offensive variation 1-3-5-2 originated from the defensive 1-5-3-2. Germany won the 1990 World Cup title with this formation under Coach Franz Beckenbauer.

Along with the 1-4-3-2-1, Italy used the 1-5-3-2 for defense during the 2012 European Championships, whereby the offensive variation 1-3-5-2 was used for most offensive movements.

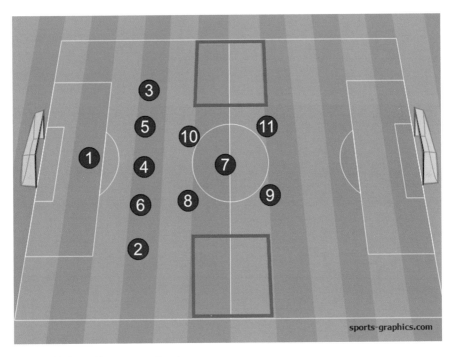

sports-graphics.com

1-5-3-2 with the problem zones on the wings

In conjunction with the illustration of the 1-3-5-2, we first focus on formations with a back three followed by a more detailed explanation of the 1-3-5-2 and the 1-3-4-3.

CHAPTER 15

Systems of Play
with the Back Three

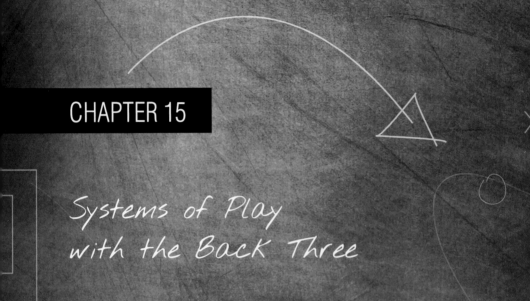

CHAPTER 15

Systems of Play with the Back Three

"Soccer was made for the attack. That is why it is good that some of our teams choose a system with three defenders that facilitates the offensive spectacle."

Arrigo Sacchi, Champions League winner and soccer revolutionary

3 backs
to increase
a attack

*T*oday many coaches only use the back three when there is a goal deficit close to the end of the game.

But another option here would be to move the two wing players up and pull a defensive midfielder back between them.

A system of play with the back three, thus, has much more to offer than just being used when there is a goal deficit.

Note that systems of play with the back three are recently becoming more popular.

For example, at the 2010 World Cup, Chile, under Coach Marcelo Bielsa, made a very strong showing with the 1-3-5-2 in South Africa.

At the 2012 European Championships, Italy even made it to the final with a nominal back three, even as the negative interpretation of critics referred to it as a defensive back five. *When to use it*

Surely the most prominent example is FC Barcelona, who continues to encounter opponents who defend extremely deep and so uses the advantages of a back three.

Because an additional player is available in the midfield, a well-functioning back three makes it possible to constantly create superior number situations against traditional systems of play, such as the 1-4-4-2.

The essential thing here, as is so often the case, is finding the right types of players who are good at 1v1 play and have tactical skills in addition to excellent technical abilities. Even in elite soccer, this is a rare combination.

Back 4
When a team works with a back four, the defensive players are continuously protecting each other and forming *defensive triangles*, whereby they play from a slightly graduated depth.

Back 3
Defending against an opponent in a back three, however, is much more direct, and inflexible and slower types of players are absolutely unsuitable for this system of play.

The wing players become very important when using a back three.

The wing players must be strong runners because they have to cover their respective sides almost entirely on their own, without support.

As an alternative, the outside players could be pulled back, but that would result in a back five instead of back three, which is contrary to this system's underlying idea.

Another reason for using the back three is when playing against a team that uses two strikers.

Today, many back fours are used to play against only one striker when covering is not too problematic.

But when a team plays with two strikers, it evens out the numbers in the defensive center, and players are often not sure how to handle this.

This system becomes dangerous when the opponent plays with three strikers, such as a 1-4-3-3, who are good 1v1 players, because here the three defenders have to handle the 1v1 situations without cover. This is why many teams use a back four with a floating player where the on-ball outside midfielder strengthens the line of three in order to double the three attackers and allows the defenders to cover each other.

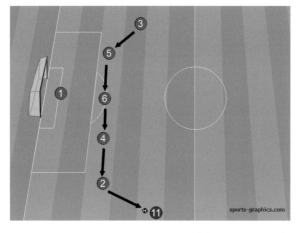

Back four with floating player

But coaches are also using a dynamic line of three in offense more frequently.

In doing so, the central midfielder drops back while the central defender goes wide and the wingbacks push up, forcing the opponent back into their own half.

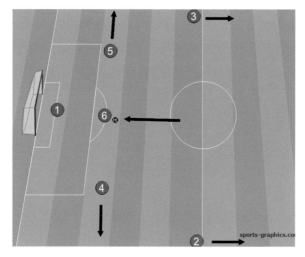

Example 1 of a dynamic line of three during build-up: The central midfielder drops back between the two central defenders.

Another option to create a superior number during build-up with a dynamic line of three is for the central midfielder to drop back between a wingback and a central defender.

An example for this is Bastian Schweinsteiger, who can often be seen using this variation on the German national team.

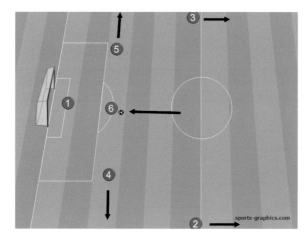

Example 2 of a dynamic line of three during build-up: The central midfielder drops back between a wingback and a central defender.

Another advantage of this dynamic line of three is that three players protect the center during a possible turnover.

Pep Guardiola also uses the dynamic line of three with Bayern Munich, as he did with FC Barcelona. In most cases, Philipp Lahm plays the position of the central midfielder who drops back. But the dynamic line of three is also often employed by Bayer Leverkusen and SC Freiburg under Christian Streich.

15.1 1-3-5-2

Juventus FC in Turin under Coach Antonio Conte is currently very successful with a 1-3-5-2-formation and won 49 consecutive games in the Serie A.

After many teams played with only two or even one striker in the past, there was the obvious consideration of placing an additional player in the midfield to generate more pressure against the opposing goal.

Along with many other teams, the German national team, in particular, was able to celebrate many successes with the 1-3-5-2, such as the 1990 World Cup victory in Italy.

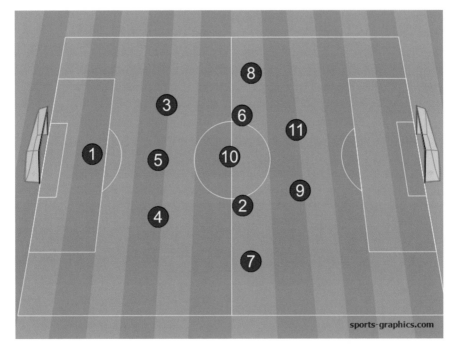

sports-graphics.com

1-3-5-2

The major advantage of the 1-3-5-2 is the maximum number of possible triangle formations of all systems, which facilitates a good short passing game.

Additionally, the midfield is nominally well covered with five players, putting very good pressure on the ball.

Furthermore, this formation has proven very successful in youth soccer when they play their first 11v11, because the structure and tasks are very clear-cut.

The biggest problem is that a line of three cannot possibly cover the entire width of the field where there is often open space for attacks from the opponent.

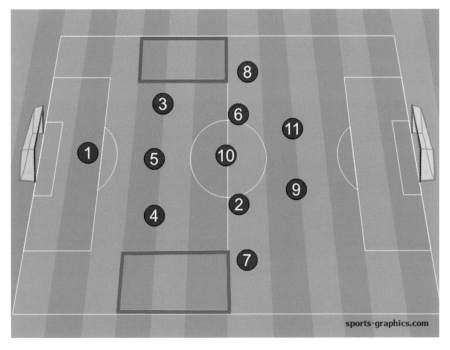

Problem areas in the 1-3-5-2

For instance, when a 1-3-5-2 encounters a 1-4-3-3, the system almost inevitably has to be changed during defensive play.

Moreover, this system lacks the typical wing players, limiting the possibilities in spite of the superior number in the midfield.

ADVANTAGES AND DISADVANTAGES OF THE 1-3-5-2

Advantages

- Superior numbers in the midfield.
- Many offensive options.
- Many possible triangle and diamond formations.
- Facilitates a good short passing game.
- Exceptionally well suited to midfield pressing because five players are available in the midfield.

Disadvantages

- Not very practical against teams with one striker.
- Places extremely high demands on players, particularly the line of three.
- The line of three cannot cover the entire width of the field.
- Hardly any advances made by the wingbacks.

15.2 1-3-4-3

The most well-known example of the 1-3-4-3 was FC Barcelona under Johan Cruyff, who had many successes with this system in the late 1980s and early 1990s.

But the even more successful Barcelona coach, student of Johan Cruyff and current FC Bayern Munich coach, Pep Guardiola, also is a proponent of the 1-3-4-3. Guardiola even resorts to the more offensive 1-3-3-4 during offensive play.

Another example for good execution of the 1-3-4-3 is the South Korean national team who placed a terrific fourth at the 2002 World Cup with this system and some refreshing offensive soccer.

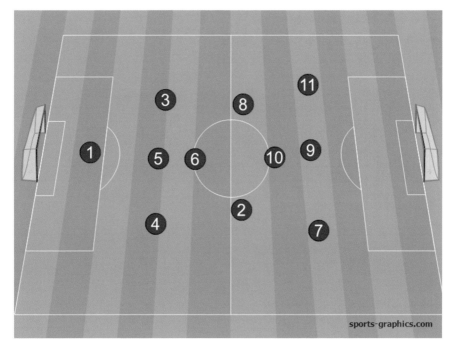

sports-graphics.com

1-3-4-3

As is the case with all systems with a line of three, the 1-3-4-3 also has an offensive orientation.

When a team works with this system, the diamond is almost always used in the midfield to achieve good graduated depth and to put pressure on the opponent.

Because of the constant superior numbers near the ball, the 1-3-4-3 also facilitates good implementation of attacking-third press and counter-press.

When the opposing team is able to extricate itself from counter-pressing situations, one of the two outside midfielders has to drop back and move in to form a situational back four.

This system of play is used almost exclusively by top teams with high individual playing levels because it presupposes extremely good ball-handling skills and tactical instincts.

Demands on individual players are very important here.

Ball-handling skills are hugely important, as well as excellent tactical instincts.

The players in the line of three must be good at winning the ball as well as playing top-level soccer in order to handle relevant situations.

ADVANTAGES AND DISADVANTAGES OF THE 1-3-4-3

Advantages

- Extremely good depth graduation.
- Combined with good positional play, this results in lots of variability in the build-up.
- Advantageous with good 1v1 players.
- Teams with good playing ability are able to implement their skills.
- Guaranteed good implementation of attacking-third press and counter-press.
- High degree of compactness in the important danger zone.

Disadvantages

- The line of three cannot cover the entire width of the field.
- Formation must be changed against teams with three strikers.
- Vulnerable during counterattacks.
- Very high demands on individual playing level.
- Requires very good tactical instincts.

CHAPTER 16

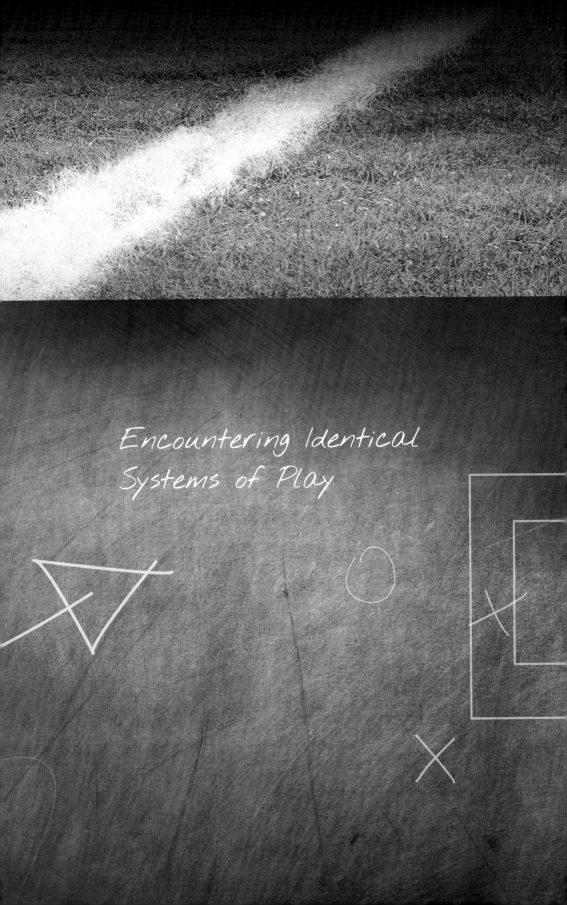

Encountering Identical
Systems of Play

CHAPTER 16

Encountering Identical Systems of Play

When two identical systems of play meet, the analysis points are nearly identical, regardless of the systems of play involved.

Next to the individual playing level of each player, a required higher running effort, as well as better timing and more accuracy and efficiency when shifting against the ball are of major importance when two identical systems of play meet.

The goal is to change the even number situations on the field into superior number situations through ball-oriented play and a high running effort.

Achieving this requires constant attempts at shifting near the ball and double- and even triple-teaming the opponent.

Another option is to switch to another system of play that creates advantages and makes it easier to even out possible weak points. So it is always beneficial when a team is able to play in different formations and systems and can be flexible.

External factors, such as home advantage or team ranking, also play an important role.

16.1 BREAKDOWN OF THE ENCOUNTER BETWEEN IDENTICAL SYSTEMS OF PLAY

BY EXAMPLE:

1-4-4-2 IN A LINE VS 1-4-4-2 IN A LINE

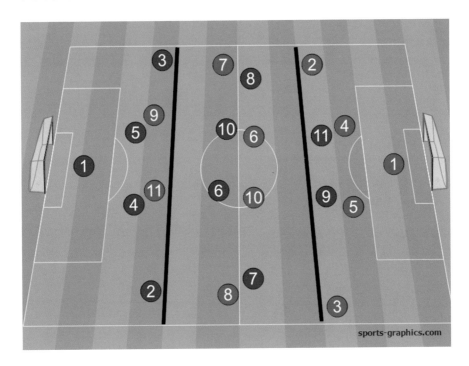

A) STARTING SITUATION

As the illustration shows, blue is in the defensive zone with a superior number ratio of 4:2.

Four blue players encounter four red players in the midfield area, resulting in an equal number situation.

In the offensive zone, the two blue attacking players encounter four red defenders.

On the wings, the two wingbacks encounter the red outside midfielders.

B) DEFENSE

It is important to establish a superior number situation in defense near the ball using good shifting movements. These shifting movements are explained in more detail with the example of two possible game situations.

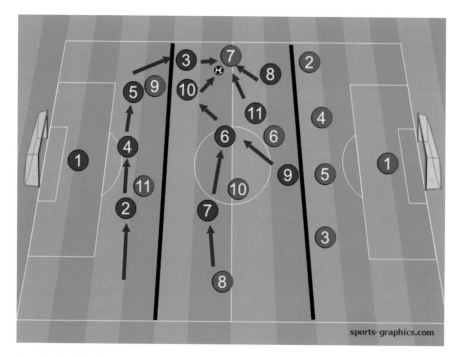

Situation 1: Ball on the wing

The red outside right midfielder receives a pass after a shift in play.

The left wingback immediately moves up to challenge the player in possession.

Ideally, he forces the player in possession to turn to the rear, where the outside midfielder pressures him, and they try to double-team and win the ball.

Here the following principle applies:

The player near the goal challenges the attacker; the player away from the goal wins the ball.

The blue number 10 tries to dribble by adding pressure from the side and at the same time blocks the passing lane of player 9 of the red team.

The blue back four has pushed through completely, still ensuring the superior number against the two red attacking players.

The blue right outside midfielder moves in, and the blue striker near the ball moves to the red 6 to prevent a return pass from 7 to 6.

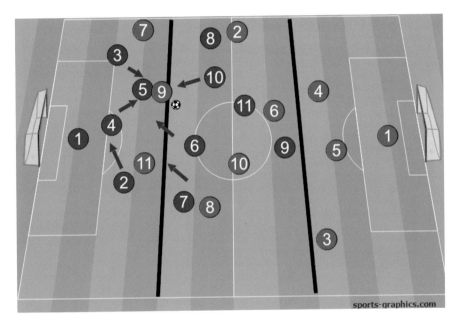

Situation 2: Ball in the center

The red attacking player 9 receives a chip pass.

The central defender near the ball steps out to challenge him.

The wingback and the off-ball central defender immediately safeguard and form a triangle defense to ensure graduated depth.

The blue player 10 immediately puts forward pressure on player 9 and actively tries to win the ball.

Player 6 comes from the side to offer support.

C) OFFENSIVE

Here the goal is to work against the opponent's shifting movements.

This can be achieved by doing the following:

- Creating space by fanning out wide and deep.
- Fast shifting play.
- Playing across lines.
- Combination play with brief ball contact.
- Chip passes to the strikers.
- Diagonal balls in behind the back four.
- Also creating superior number situations in offense, which also offers an advantage for counter-pressing during a possible turnover.

16.2 ENCOUNTER BETWEEN TWO DIFFERENT SYSTEMS OF PLAY

BY EXAMPLE:

1-4-4-2 IN A LINE VS 1-4-2-3-1

When two different systems of play encounter each other, it is very important to know where open spaces in the opponent's ranks can develop during offensive play and where possible open spaces for the opponent must be eliminated during defense.

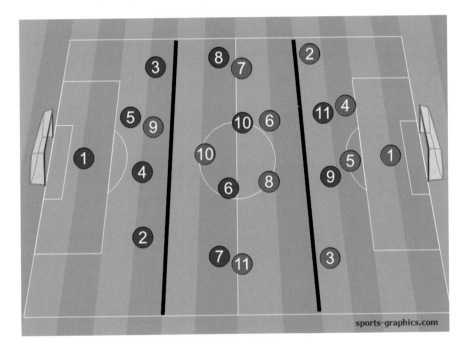

A) STARTING POSITION

In the defensive zone, the blue team has a big numbers advantage with four defensive players against one attacking player.

As a result, there is a 4:5 inferior number ratio in the midfield area.

In the offensive zone, the four red defensive players face two blue attacking players.

B) DEFENSE

Here, answering the question of how to even out the inferior number in the midfield— especially how to handle the opposing number 10—is critical during defensive play.

Because there is an extra line available with the 1-4-2-3-1-formation, it is also important that the four blue midfielders make sure they don't lose the opposing player at their back, which easily could cause lines to be crossed.

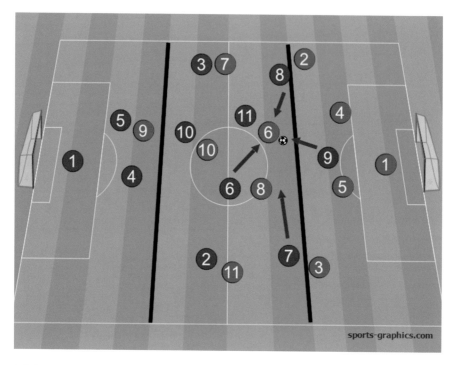

Solution 1: Dropping striker

The blue attacking player 11 near the ball drops back in the midfield area to prevent a superior number situation for the opponent.

Of course it must be understood that this can only be a situational solution because both attacking strikers most likely would not be able to sustain this major extra effort for more than 90 minutes and would also lack the strength for offensive actions.

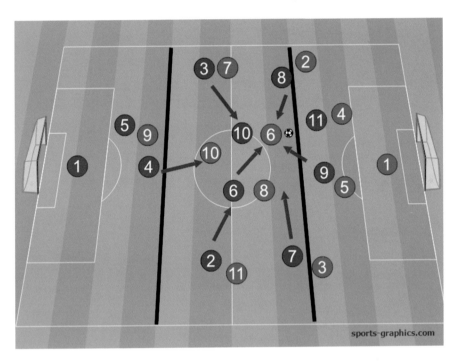

Solution 2: The central defender steps out.

If the action is bold and additional pressure is put on the opponent in the 1-4-2-3-1, one of the two central defenders shifts position toward the red player 10, pressuring to the opponent.

Exercise caution in case the opponent tries for a long ball.

In this situation, the central defender must immediately drop back to form a triangle defense with his adjacent players.

C) OFFENSE

When playing against a 1-4-2-3-1, space frequently opens up behind the two outside midfielders because these two often have a very offensive focus.

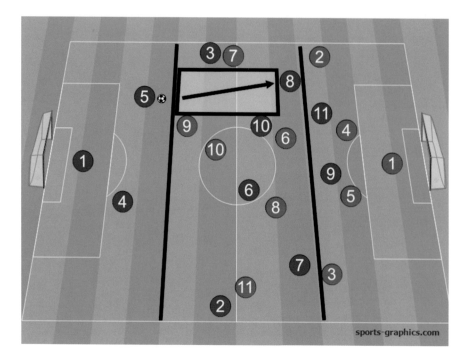

Skillful tactical behavior from the outside midfielder—who shows flexibility on his running paths and must also ask for and go to the ball in the center—is as important as good, spacious passing from the central defender.

If the blue defender near the ball then comes along, good situations often emerge for overrunning the opponent on the wing.

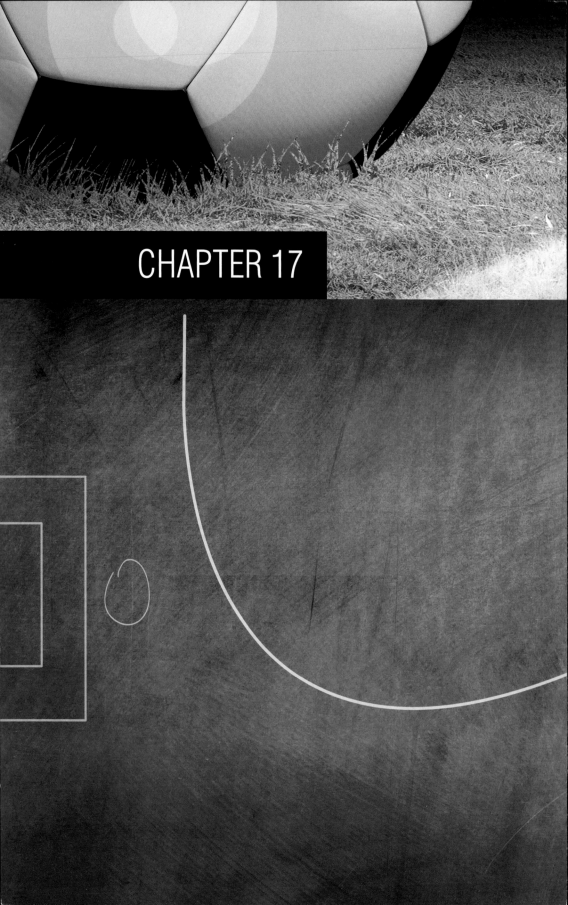

CHAPTER 17

Match Plan:
Perfect Preparation
for the Next Game

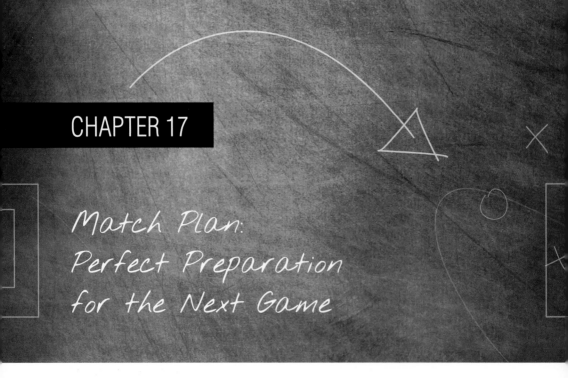

CHAPTER 17

Match Plan: Perfect Preparation for the Next Game

"What would help us is a quick goal and a quick final whistle, and maybe we could park the team bus in front of our goal."

Thomas Tuchel, former Bundesliga coach at FSV Mainz 05

From a world rankings analysis, the four game phases, the principles of zone soccer, the game concept, the tactical considerations, as well as formations and systems of play and their juxtaposition—every game requires a match plan.

German Bundesliga coach, Thomas Tuchel, often attributed their successes to a match plan, consequently placing the term *match plan* in the headlines in the German-speaking regions.

A *match plan* is a strategic measure in soccer with the purpose of

- optimally preparing a team for its next game,
- recognizing and exploiting the opponent's strengths and weaknesses, and
- optimally preparing a team for tactical changes or specific situations.

With a match plan, general principles are purposely applied to the opponent and adapted to the requirements on any given game day.

Every soccer coach's goal, regardless of his league, is to keep coincidence to an absolute minimum.

Detailed analyses of the opponent and the coach's own team and the resulting tactical implementation is used to counteract that coincidence.

Next to soccer knowledge, optimal transfer of knowledge, coaching, as well as good communication skills, it is important that each coach has a concrete plan in his head so that the tactical knowledge can be purposefully communicated.

Each coach can develop an individual match plan according to his preferences, but the following sections offer detailed lists of the most important points.

17.1 MATCH PLAN CONTENT

When creating a match plan, the coach and his team must take the following considerations into account.

- Strategic goals
> What is our long-term goal?

   Such as, for instance, reaching a certain place in the standings.

- Short-term goals
> What is the goal for the next game?

- Team analysis
> How is my team ranked right now?
> Own condition: what is my team's state of mind?
> Which tactical measures need to be employed?

- Opponent analysis
> Strength and weakness profile
> Game concept
> Tactics
> System of play
> Standard situations
> Peculiarities

- External conditions
> Field conditions
> How is the weather?
> Game location: home or away?
> Timing: what time of day is the game being played?
> Opponent's supporters
> Referee: who oversees the game?
> How does the ref generally referee a game?

When creating a match plan, the previous lists should always be closely analyzed.

Following the analysis, the coaching staff compiles a strategy for how the game can be won. An implementation plan for the training week is made based upon that strategy.

Along with the lineup and the tactical approach, a good match plan also contains individual player analyses, as well as behavior during standard situations and possible changes, depending on the course of the game.

PLAN B: IF–THEN STRATEGIES

A plan B should also be in place so specific changes can be made if the game moves in an unwanted direction.

Of course, match plans are much more difficult to create in amateur sports, because in those games, decisions are often based on third person observations or one's own insights from watched games.

But here, too, it makes absolute sense to know the most important points, such as game concept, tactical focus, standard situations, as well as the opponent's key players, to be able to take appropriate counter measures.

17.2   ANALYZING THE OPPONENT

The most important point in a match plan is most certainly the opponent analysis.

When analyzing the opponent, the following points must be examined to be able to make deductions for a match plan:

- What is the opponents' game concept?
- How does he behave in the four game phases?
- Defensive tactics.
- Offensive tactics.
- Individual tactics.
- Group tactics.
- Team tactics.
- Game tactics.
- Behavior in standard situations.

It is absolutely necessary to develop a match plan for offense and a separate plan for defense based on these points of the opponent analysis.

Depending on the opponent, the focus will either be more on offense or defense.

17.2.1   WHAT IS THE OPPONENT'S GAME CONCEPT?

- Long balls or short passes?
- Counter tactics or possession play?
- Young team, old team, mixed?
- Experienced or inexperienced?
- Cultural background/club identity
- Aggressive or restrained?
- Offensive or defensive?
- Homegrown talent or foreign purchase?
- > **Fundamental question:**

What is the best way to counter the opponent's game concept?

17.2.2 ANALYZING INDIVIDUAL OFFENSIVE TACTICS

While observing the opponent, the offensive behavior of individual players is analyzed with respect to individual tactics.

*   In doing so, the following points must be taken into account:
*   Opponent's strengths and weaknesses in the area of individual offensive tactics.
*   Are there outstanding individual players?
*   If so, what are their offensive strengths?
*   How can I counter these strengths?
*   Which of my players are best suited to face this player?
*   Are there peculiarities; for instance, does the opponent use a special trick?

17.2.3 ANALYZING INDIVIDUAL DEFENSIVE TACTICS

This point focuses on the specific analysis of the opponent's weaknesses in the area of defense that can be exploited.

The following points must be scrutinized:
*   What are the individual weaknesses in defense?
*   What are the individual strengths?
*   Is there a particularly slow opposing player?
*   Which is the opponent's weak side on defense?
*   What are the physical and athletic qualifications?
*   What is the opponent's mental state?

17.2.4 ANALYZING GROUP OFFENSIVE TACTICS

When analyzing the opponent's group tactics during offensive play, the following points must be taken into account:

- What are the opponent's strengths and weaknesses with respect to group tactics in attacking play on offense?
- What type of group tactics does the opponent employ during offensive play?
- What does the opponent's wing play look like?
- What is the opponent's behavior when playing through the center?
- How does the opponent execute shifting play?
- Are there specific attack triggers?

17.2.5 ANALYZING GROUP DEFENSIVE TACTICS

Which group tactics can I use to cause the opponent trouble during defensive play?

- Where are the strengths and where are the weak points in the opponent's group tactics during defense?
- How does the opponent move within the individual team sections?
- Which of the following options are appropriate against the approaching opponent:
    - **Wing play**
    - **Play though the center**
    - **Third man play**
    - **Combination play**
    - **Quick shifting play**

17.2.6 ANALYZING TEAM OFFENSIVE TACTICS

When examining team tactics, the opponent's formation and the opposing system are extremely important:

- What are the strengths and weaknesses of this system?
- What is the opponent's offensive formation, and how does he interpret this system during possession?
- Where could our system have problems against the opponent's system?
- How can we fix these problems?
- Could we possibly have to switch to another system?
- Can the opponent switch to another system?
- How does the opponent switch from offense to defense?
- Is the opponent able to determine changes in the rhythm of play?

17.2.7 ANALYZING TEAM DEFENSIVE TACTICS

When analyzing the opponent's team defensive tactics, the following points are very important:

- In which zone does the opponent defend?
- Which defensive strategies are used?
- Do they play offside?
- How do the individual team sections work together?
- Can I confuse the opponent by changing the rhythm of play?
- What will our pace be?
- How does the opponent switch from offense to defense?

17.3 ANALYZING THE OPPONENT IN STANDARD SITUATIONS

Standard situations play a very important role in modern soccer.

On the international level, 20% of all goals are scored after standard situations. In many top leagues, that rate is much higher.

Standard situations represent an important part of the opponent analysis because counter measures against standard situations are easy to practice, and surprises can be avoided if the opponent's more unusual variations are known.

Offensive variation patterns can be easily practiced with the *inactive ball*.

In a match plan, the following standard situations should be examined from a defensive and offensive point of view:

- Kick-off
- Free kick
- Throw-in
- Penalty kick
- Corner kick

17.3.1 KICK-OFF

Two teams just before kick-off

A kick-off can take place by the opponent at the start of a game, after halftime, or with a scored goal.

Next to rehearsed variations, the kick-off is also interesting from a psychological point of view.

A kick-off into the opponent's half can be a deliberate sign that the team is not intimidated.

A) OPPONENT ANALYSIS OF OFFENSIVE KICK-OFF

The following points must be analyzed:
- Are there rehearsed kick-off patterns?
- What do these patterns look like?
- Do they differ with different kick-off situations?

B) OPPONENT ANALYSIS OF DEFENSIVE KICK-OFF

- Can I surprise the opponent during kick-off?
- Based on psychological principles, do I purposely play forward during kick-off?

17.3.2 FREE KICK

More than a few soccer games are decided by free kicks.

Be it by players with outstanding shooting technique, such as David Beckham or Juninho, rehearsed variations that take the opponent by surprise, or high balls that are exploited by excellent head ball players.

Free kick by

Bastian Schweinsteiger

When analyzing free kicks, it is important to first identify behavior during free kicks relative to the location where the free kick will be taken (e.g., free kicks from the side or at various distances from the goal) and then to identify the opponent's behavior toward the defense, and on offense, to detect weaknesses in the opponent's defense in order to derive opportunities for the own team.

A) OPPONENT ANALYSIS OF OFFENSIVE FREE KICKS

- How are free kicks taken from the side?
- How are they taken from the center?
- How does the opponent take free kicks at different distances from the goal?
- Does the opponent have special free kick variations?
- Who are the shooters?
- Who runs to the ball?
- Is there a player who takes an outstanding direct kick?
- Are there excellent head ball players?

B) OPPONENT ANALYSIS OF DEFENSIVE FREE KICKS

- Where are the opponent's defensive weaknesses during free kicks?
- How can I exploit these weaknesses?
- Does the goalie have a weak spot?
- How does the goalie command the penalty box?
- Can I purposely block one of the opponent's strong players?
- How does the opponent form the wall?
- Does the wall jump during free kicks?
- Does the opponent defend free kicks using a 1v1 defense, zone defense, or a mix of the two?

17.3.3 CORNER

Mesut Özil taking a corner

In soccer, corners have always been a promising means for scoring a goal and are becoming increasingly more important because of the outstanding advancement in defensive strategies that make goals from open play more difficult.

The player taking the corner cannot be attacked and thus can play the ball into the danger zone virtually unimpeded.

In addition, shooting techniques continue to improve, the ball's trajectory is increasingly more difficult to predict, and, as previously mentioned, head ball soccer has greatly evolved.

There are many different variations possible in offensive play. Corner kicks are often played short against teams with good head ball skills, like, for instance, FC Barcelona often does.

Teams with strong head ball skills and tall players rehearse specific variations that allow them to take advantage of these strengths in the air. One variation that is gaining more popularity was taken from basketball: Teams use blocking to get their strong head ball players open.

Overall, ball-oriented play has prevailed over zone defense.

An interesting subject has emerged with respect to standard situation defensive behavior, particularly corner kicks.

To date, no ideal solution has been found, which is why some teams use 1v1 defense, others take a ball-oriented approach, and still others use a combination of both variations.

sports-graphics.com

1v1 defense during corner kicks

Zone defense with corner kicks is used with the same objective as ball-oriented play from the flow of play, which is to narrow the space as much as possible to create superior number situations.

Here several players simultaneously go to the ball as it comes into the box, whereby the won ball will ideally trigger a dangerous counter.

Zone defense is used to prevent the attacking player from gaining an advantage on his approach to the ball.

The best head ball players are able to go up against the ball from the danger zones, reducing the risk of the ball ending up behind the defenders.

Zone defense during corner kicks; example of formation with zone defense during a corner

PROVEN STRUCTURE FOR ZONE DEFENSE DURING CORNER KICKS

- The two central defenders stand in the middle of the 5-yard line.
- The wingbacks stand between the posts and the 5-yard line.
- The on-ball outside midfielder positions so he can step in if there is a short corner.
- Three strong head ball players are positioned near the 12-yard line and form a triangle.
- Another player is positioned on the 18-yard line to block shots from the second row and to initiate a counterattack.
- The attacking player is positioned in the center circle and from there aligns with the ball.

A) ADVANTAGES OF ZONE DEFENSE WITH CORNER KICKS

- Narrows spaces.
- Positions strong head ball players in danger zones.
- Places superior number near the ball.
- The ability to defend regardless of the opponent's head ball abilities, because the strongest head ball players are always in the most dangerous spaces.
- Lower likelihood of a ball being slipped in.
- Lower likelihood of a penalty kick because of less yanking, pushing, and pulling.

B) DISADVANTAGES OF ZONE DEFENSE WITH CORNER KICKS

- Players often don't go to the ball and stand in their zones.
- Strong head ball players encounter less strong head ball players in less dangerous areas and from there try to put the second ball into the danger zone directly in front of the goal.
- The goal line is no longer occupied to ensure a superior number in the dangerous spaces, which is why it is important for the players to win 1v1 duels.
- Many strong attacking head ball players prefer going up against a purely zone defense instead of a 1v1 defense because they don't have to focus on the run-up and an opposing player, but rather only on the ball, which allows them to go up against the balls with even more speed.

C) OPPONENT ANALYSIS OF THE CORNER KICKS DURING OFFENSIVE PLAY

- How does the opponent act?
- What are the opponent's variations?
- What do these variations look like?
- Are there strong head ball players?
- Are there strong shooters?
- Does the shooter cut the ball toward the goal or away from it?

D) OPPONENT ANALYSIS OF THE CORNER KICKS DURING DEFENSIVE PLAY

- How does the opponent defend corner kicks?
- Zone defense, 1v1 defense, or a combination of the two?
- How many players stand at the goal posts?
- Where are the opponent's weak spots; where is he strong?
- Is it possible to play short corners?
- What is the goalie's command of the goal?

17.3.4 THROW-IN

Improved throw-in behavior brings much potential to soccer and overall is much undervalued.

During a German Bundesliga game there are on average more than 50 throw-ins, meaning they take place more often than every two minutes.

The problem is that the thrower's playing options are limited by the touchline behind him because this only allows him a 180-degree angle to continue play rather than a 360-degree angle.

Throw-in by FC Bayern Munich captain Philipp Lahm

A) THROW-IN FOR THE OPPONENT

A throw-in by the opponent offers an ideal opportunity for a situational pressing, because the interruption in play and the ball-oriented shifting into the zone of the throw-in creates opportunity for superior number situations to narrow spaces, putting pressure on the opponent.

Quick throw-ins can be prevented by "sandwiching" the oncoming player.

Preventing a quick throw-in by "sandwiching" the oncoming player

B) THROW-IN FOR ONE'S OWN TEAM

The objective for a throw-in of one's own team is to continue the game as quickly as possible so the opponent does not time to block the spaces.

If this cannot be prevented, it is important to then create a superior number near the ball.

The players must now make a coordinated effort to get open.

By quickly shifting play or opening up spaces, the situation can essentially be exploited with a player near the ball opening a space and the off-ball player pushing into the now open space.

It is important that the player asking for the ball does not get too close to the thrower because often the ball can then only be returned hard from a short distance, and the thrower is immediately under pressure.

If the thrower is completely blocked in and these two variations are not possible, the ball is thrown down the line where a player is waiting to receive the ball, to dig in against the opposing player and hold the ball, or to get a free kick.

Players often forget that there is no offside with a throw-in, meaning a player in an offside position can receive the ball from a throw-in.

In recent years, dangerous scenarios created by long throw-ins into the penalty area have become more prevalent.

Players such as Christian Fuchs from the Austrian national team or Rory Delap of Stoke City can execute a throw-in like a cross, particularly with throw-ins near the backline.

Studies show that throwing the ball as far as possible requires a relatively low release angle of ideally 30 degrees to 45 degrees. This generates the highest possible velocity, which in turn benefits the distance.

Skillful positioning and strong head ball players can make these throw-ins extremely dangerous.

C) OPPONENT ANALYSIS OF THE THROW-IN DURING OFFENSIVE PLAY

- Does the opponent have a concept for throw-ins?
- If so, do they differ with the location of the throw-in?
- Are the opponent's throw-ins slow or fast?
- Which player does the throw-in?
- Does the opponent have a player who can throw in especially far?

D) OPPONENT ANALYSIS OF THE THROW-IN DURING DEFENSIVE PLAY

- Does the opponent quickly block with a throw-in?
- Is it possible to do a throw-in close to the goal?
- Which variations are suitable?
- Does the opponent possibly drop way back so the throw-in can be done to the rear?

17.3.5 PENALTY KICK

Many important games are decided by a penalty kick or a penalty shootout.

Good luck and bad luck often live side by side.

Or maybe not...

Statistically speaking, the likelihood of the shooter scoring on the penalty kick is 75%.

By now, numerous studies have disproven the many myths surrounding the penalty kick.

There are, for instance, no indications that the fouled player should not take the shot.

The assertion that the player who feels best should take the penalty kick also cannot possibly be true because how does anyone know how the other players are feeling?

With respect to goalies, it can be said that their reactions are always better with analyses of the opposing shooters. The best known example is Jens Lehmann at the 2006 World Cup, who was given a note with the important information regarding the shooters just before the penalty shootout against Argentina.

Some goalies try to confuse the shooter by wildly moving their arms up and down.

The Spanish national team goalie Pepe Reina lets his upper body fall forward just before the shot to shorten the opponent's angle.

Messi positions the ball prior to a penalty kick

The following points help the shooter with the successful execution of a penalty kick:

- Visualizing: On the way to taking the penalty kick, think about how to exploit the ball.
- Block out all disturbing factors and focus only on the penalty kick.
- Inconspicuously set your sights on the target and completely ignore the goalie.
- A short run-up of four to six steps is recommended.
- Do not change the target and take the penalty kick immediately after the referee's whistle.
- Statistically speaking, the shot should be quick and high in one of the two corners.
- It is advantageous to know the goalie's weak side. According to statistics, it is most often the left side because the percentage of lefthanders is significantly lower.
- A shot with the inside of the foot is preferable because the larger contact area ensures more certainty and accuracy.

- Another popular variation is to trick the goalie, as, for example, Andrea Pirlo did with a chip ball at the 2012 European Championships. But this requires extremely steady nerves and great skill.

By the way, it is important to know that the offside rule applies to the penalty kick, which is why the offensive players should not position themselves any closer to the 18-yard line than the opponent's last defender in order to exploit rebounds.

And as is true with everything else, here, too: Practice makes perfect!

A) OPPONENT ANALYSIS OF THE PENALTY KICK DURING OFFENSIVE PLAY

- Who takes the penalty kick?
- Where will he shoot the ball?
- How does he shoot the ball?
- Did the shooter possibly miss a penalty kick in the last game?
- Does the shooter have a ritual? If so, can I break his ritual?

B) OPPONENT ANALYSIS OF THE PENALTY KICK DURING DEFENSIVE PLAY

- Who are my potential shooters?
- Who is in good shape?
- Depending on the score, possibly change the shooter to, for instance, protect a player.
- Peculiarities of the opposing goalie.
- Goalie's weak side

17.4 PLAN B: IF–THEN STRATEGIES

Every coach must adjust to unplanned positive and negative changes and have a plan B, so he can immediately switch gears without unsettling the team.

If–then strategies should absolutely be discussed and practiced with the team in advance.

The following are the most important scenarios that can occur:

- Injured players
- Red cards
- No more subs
- Change of formation
- Change of system of play
- Point deficit
- Maintaining the lead until the end of the game
- Coach is ordered off the field
- No back-up goalie
- Penalty shootout

17.5   PLAN B: SUPERIOR AND INFERIOR NUMBER SITUATIONS

"After the opponent's red card we played worse than we did before, and we were unable to pressure the opponent in spite of their inferior number!"

Inferior and superior situations are an important form of if–when strategies.

It often happens that coaches are forced to react to inferior or superior situations because of red cards.

Of course, a good match plan takes this point into account.

Above all, it is important to stay calm and not make hasty decisions.

Also important are, of course, the game score, the opponent's strength, and the team's ability to successfully tackle 1v1 situations.

SITUATION 1: SUPERIOR NUMBER OF ONE'S OWN TEAM

For the team with one extra player, it is now even more important to fan out across the width and depth of the field.

In addition, the strikers must continue to go offside behind the back four and, of course, also leave the offside position early enough in order to push the opponent into his own half.

Furthermore, this behavior by the strikers causes confusion in the opponent's defensive line.

Now there is space for the team's back four, who try to build up pressure with the two wingbacks that are pushed way up for this purpose.

These measures cause the opponent's back four to unavoidably be pushed far back into their own half.

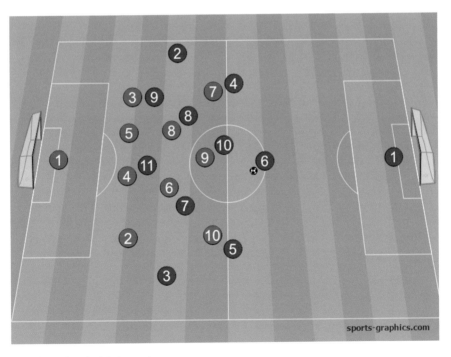

The red team has the inferior number

A faster pace with brief touches now becomes more important during build-up, as well as playing across stations and lines, which can put lots of pressure on the opponent.

Gaps will inevitably open up at some point, and they must then be calmly exploited.

Players will continuously attempt to break through across the wings with the wingbacks that are positioned up high in order to score a goal.

Playing across the wings is preferable to playing through the middle because there the defending team tries to maintain a superior number and protect the center.

SITUATION 2: INFERIOR NUMBER OF ONE'S OWN TEAM

What do I do when my team loses a player?

This can happen because of a red card, a lack of subs, or when all of the subs have been used.

The question then arises: Which position did the player occupy, and what is the current score?

A point deficit represents a much greater challenge for a team because now there is only one attacking player to put pressure on the opponent, because exerting pressure with multiple attackers simultaneously would open up large holes in the defense.

One possibility would be a substitution to add a fresh player with strong running skills. Another option would be to change the system of play.

In this situation, it is generally recommended to just play with one striker and to drop back, which, for the moment, does not result in any serious changes in defensive play.

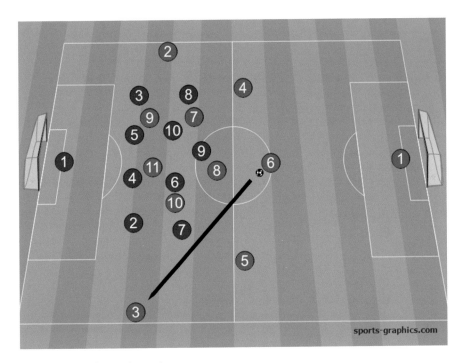

The red team has the superior number.

The number of players in the team's half is still the same as before the loss of one player.

If the opponent does not react with a substitution or a system change, nothing seriously changes in defensive play except that the team would usually have to go deeper.

Most important is that the single striker no longer puts any pressure on the opponent's back four but rather remains attached to the defending unit.

For the record, inferior and superior number situations should always be practiced in training as preparation for an emergency.

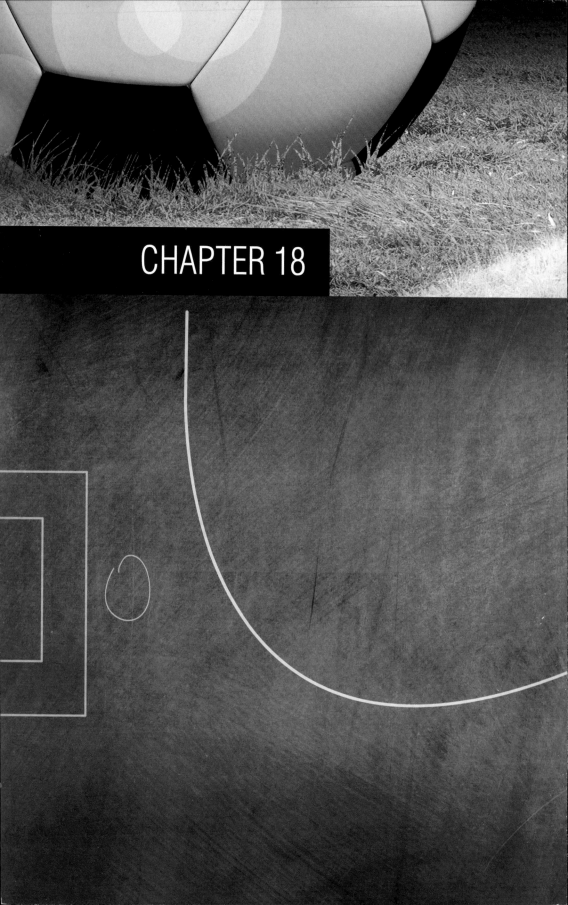

CHAPTER 18

Model Match Plan

CHAPTER 18

Model Match Plan

The following pages offer a practically relevant draft of a model match plan.

To this purpose we simulate a scenario.

Starting position

Our upper-level amateur team of many young and hungry players is playing an important semi-final game for the league championship, which, if won, may result in the lucrative and prestigious participation in the German Soccer Association Cup.

The opposing team is strong with many technically- and individually-skilled players that compete at the next higher level.

The opposing team is positioned in the secured midfield and masterfully won the last regular season game.

After watching this game and using lots of information from other coaches and the Internet, the coaching staff has worked out strengths and weaknesses and incorporated them into a match plan.

18.1 GENERAL POINTS

* Strategic goals

Winning the league championship and qualifiying for the German Soccer Association Cup was given as a single goal prior to the season.

* Short-term goals

Winning and, thereby, moving on to the next round.

* Team analysis

After a rocky start to the season, our team is in optimal physical shape and shows a definite upward trend.

The last league game against a strong opponent who behaved similarly to the upcoming opponent was easily won, boosting morale.

Intensity and participation in training units are very high.

There are no injured or suspended players.

* Analysis of external factors

The game will be an away game on Saturday, played on the opponent's large, well-groomed field.

The opponent was able to win most of the points at home and has many spectators who will support the home team.

The weather forecast predicts hot temperatures above 86 °F, so hydration will be important.

The game will be overseen by a team of experienced referees.

A busload of fans will be there to support the away team.

In general

The opponent analysis shows that the opponent has trouble with teams that play aggressively, put constant pressure on the opponent, and press early. It will become difficult if the team pulls back too far and allows the opponent to play.

18.2 HOW DOES THE OPPONENT
BEHAVE DURING THE FOUR PHASES OF PLAY?

PHASE 1 ANALYSIS:
OWN TEAM'S POSSESSION/OPPONENT IS ORGANIZED

- The opponent plays with a rehearsed midfield press, which, depending on the situation, changes to attacking-third press.

> **Solution:** Pointing out possible solutions to counter these pressing strategies. Along with an "anti-pressing ball," a diagonal shift in play against the shifting movement can also be promising because the off-ball players also move far to the center during an attacking-third press.

- During offensive play, we will be in a diamond formation. Here it will be important to put pressure on the opponent.

> **Solution:** The players on the outside of the diamond push way up, rendering the opponent's back four completely ineffective. Now the opponent's central midfielder has to drop back to even out the numbers, which creates open spaces in the midfield.

> Moreover, if the ball is moved quickly, spaces will continue to open up on the wings where superior number situations develop.

PHASE 2 ANALYSIS:
OPPONENT HAS POSSESSION/OWN TEAM IS DISORGANIZED

- Once the opponent wins the ball, he will use rehearsed behaviors to score a goal as quickly as possible.

- The outside players immediately get involved in attacking play, fan out widely, and wait for a long ball to be able to quickly move toward the goal.

> **Solution:** Very important here is extremely good shifting play on defense, and one of the two central midfielders must always systematically hold the position to protect the back four and preferably not get into a counterattack situation.

> Moreover, it is important to engage in counter-pressing whenever the situation permits in order to prevent a quick continuation of play.

PHASE 3 ANALYSIS:
OPPONENT HAS POSSESSION/OWN TEAM IS ORGANIZED

- When the opponent plays against a well-organized team, offensively it either tries to bring the flanks, who are strong 1v1 players, into the game, or it tries to play across its opponent's lines.
> **Solution:** The player in possession must be pressured continuously. We will, therefore, put pressure on the opponent with a midfield press that will change based on the situation over to an attacking-third press, as far up in the own team's half as possible and try to set a very fast pace.
> In addition, we will try to create superior number situations with very good shifting movements, which makes it possible to persistently double-team on the wing.
> Moreover, good graduated depth must be ensured by constantly forming triangles to keep the opponent from playing across lines.
- Often the two outside defenders try to engage the opponent, whereupon the two wing players shift their focus to the center to open up space on the flank.
> **Solution:** Timely transfer of the outside midfielder and blocking of the outside defender.
- Whenever possible, the goal kick will be short, so the combination soccer strengths can be used.
> **Solution:** Systematic blocking during the goal kick to force the opponent to play long balls where we are superior.

PHASE 4 ANALYSIS:

OWN TEAM'S POSSESSION/OPPONENT IS UNORGANIZED

- Defensive shifting is one of the weak points.
- > **Solution:** Practice offensive shifting, and simulate counteractions in training.
- The two outside strikers do not shift consistently enough, particularly on the wings, during defensive play.
- > **Solution:** When gaining possession, the first ball should be played into the open spaces on the wings.
- Whenever possible the opponent tries to quickly recapture the ball in counter-pressing.
- > **Solution:** Constant superior numbers near the ball and doing a quick shifting of play to the wing against the movements.

18.3 TACTICAL ANALYSIS

A) 1-4-4-2 VS 1-4-3-3

Starting position

An opponent who plays with a 1-4-3-3 always has strong offensive players, a high individual skill level on the wings, and will try to capture the ball with an early press.

When comparing the two formations with the aid of the zone soccer model, the following facts can be ascertained:

- The own team's back four has a 4-3 number advantage.
- Our midfield has a 2-3 number disadvantage in the midfield.
- There are equal numbers on the flanks.
- The two forwards face two central defenders.

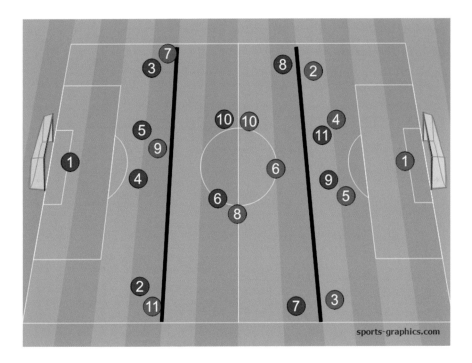

sports-graphics.com

B) DEFENSIVE TACTICAL ANALYSIS

- Individually strong players on the wings
- > **Solution:** Optimal shifting and teamwork by the two wing players creates superior number situations on the wing.
- Inferior number in the center midfield
- > **Solution 1:** In the forward zone, the two strikers in the center must drop back and focus on the opponent's central midfielder.
- > **Solution 2:** In the midfield area, the on-ball outside midfielder pushes to the center.
- > **Solution 3:** Always stand deep enough so that a pass to the opposing central midfielder never goes past the forward-most defending line.
- Problem: Lines can be bridged with deep, vertical passes.
- > **Solution:** The midfield must make sure that the opponent doesn't break away from behind. Moreover, good triangulation and safeguarding is a must for every long pass.

During defensive play, defense, midfield, and offense should not be lined up in a row but ideally staggered in a way that covers all the gaps.

- Problem: Early pressing by the opponent.
- > **Solution:** During an extreme press, a chip ball is played to the two forwards or a diagonal ball to the outside midfielder against the opponent's shifting movements.

C) OFFENSIVE TACTICAL ANALYSIS

Possible chances

- Only five of the opponent's outfield players think defensively. When the midfield sides don't contribute enough, inferior number situations will inevitably occur.
- > **Chance:** Quick shift in play to offense.
- Usually, during a turnover while moving forward in the midfield, the opponent is almost always at a numbers disadvantage.
- > Chance: Quick, deep vertical balls to quickly exploit the inferior number situation.
- Often the opponent's offensive wing players don't contribute enough on defense.
- > **Chance:** Get the outside midfielders open with a quick shift in play to the own team's wings.
- Changing from 1-4-4-2 line to 1-4-4-2 diamond during offensive play
- > **Chance:** Use the advantages of the diamond. The two strikers and the three offensive midfielders provide five offensive players who can put lots of pressure on the opposing defensive unit.
- Important: The key will be the smooth transition from the line formation during defense to the diamond formation on offense and extremely good shifting behavior in both directions.

18.4 ANALYZING THE OPPONENT IN STANDARD SITUATIONS

A) OPPONENT ANALYSIS: DEFENDING PASSING

- With the kick-off, the opponent immediately tries to put pressure on the ball.
- > **Solution:** A wide diagonal ball in behind against the shifting movement, which also signals that even as a bush-league team at an away game, we will play fearlessly.

B) OPPONENT ANALYSIS: ATTACKING PASSING

- The opponent tries to bring the wings into the game diagonally with the first ball.
- > **Solution:** Timely deep-staggered formation and double-teaming on the wing.
- After being scored on, negative body language is often noticeable during the kick-off.
- > **Solution:** Immediately going back to the ball after a possible goal.

C) OPPONENT ANALYSIS: DEFENDING FREE KICK

- During defense, the opponent plays zone defense and has trouble with high balls.
- > **Solution:** Hard, high balls into the open spaces of the zone defense, whereby our players will move into these spaces with coordinated running behavior and speed.
- It is obvious that the opponent only puts one player into the wall during free kicks from the side, even when two opposing players are near the ball.
- > **Solution:** Based on the situation, take short free kicks to exploit the superior number situation.

D) OPPONENT ANALYSIS: ATTACKING FREE KICK

- The opponent has good shooters and nearly all of their indirect free kicks are played short.
- > **Solution:** Superior numbers near the ball during free kicks and avoiding free kicks near the goal.
- There were no discernible special, surprising variations.

E) OPPONENT ANALYSIS: DEFENDING CORNER

- Here, too, the opponent uses zone defense.
- > **Solution:** High, hard balls into the spaces that our strong head ball players run to.

F) OPPONENT ANALYSIS: ATTACKING CORNER

- The opponent tries to take all corners short.
- > **Solution:** Create superior numbers near the ball to apply immediate pressure.

G) OPPONENT ANALYSIS: DEFENDING THROW-IN

- During throw-ins, the opponent executes constant, situational pressing and immediately tries to block spaces.
- > **Solution:** This makes it important to keep the ball in play and to otherwise execute the throw-in as quickly as possible.
- Level with the penalty box, both wingbacks who can throw far try to throw the ball to the two strong head ball-playing strikers, who flick the ball to the second post, were two fast players will be at the ready.

H) OPPONENT ANALYSIS: ATTACKING THROW-IN

- The opponent tries to execute quick throw-ins and always throws the ball to a player's foot.
- > **Solution:** Blocking spaces and not allowing the opponent to square up to the goal during offense.

I) OPPONENT ANALYSIS: DEFENDING PENALTY KICK

The opponent has many experienced penalty kick shooters.

But after multiple observations it has been determined that they always follow the same patterns that were ascertained.

> **Solution:** The goalkeeping coach responds to these patterns and simulates these shooters during practice.

J) OPPONENT ANALYSIS: ATTACKING PENALTY KICK

The opposing goalie is noticeably stronger on his right side and, during a penalty kick, stands on the line for a long time.

> **Solution:** All shooters who don't improvise practice the penalty kick into the shooters' left corner.

18.5 PLAN B

Because a tournament can have extra time and penalty shootouts, these scenarios were, of course, rehearsed.

Moreover, with a point deficit, the team would play much more offensively, which, of course, was practiced many times beforehand.

Suggestions were also given on how to play smart with a possible point advantage, particularly late in the game.

Here the formation would be changed to a 1-4-1-4-1 with a brawny striker who can hold the ball on his own until the rest of the team has moved up, as well as a powerful, experienced player who can fill the position between the two lines of four.

Superior and inferior number scenarios because of red cards or depleted subs are consistently addressed and practiced.

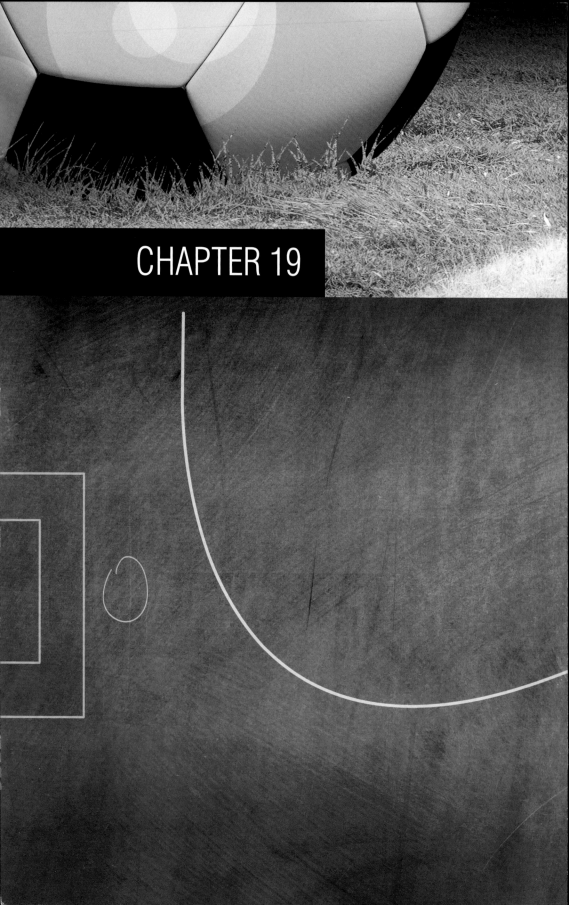

CHAPTER 19

Training Week Design

CHAPTER 19

Training Week Design

"Only knowledge that is applied is power!"

After a match plan is finalized, it is important to plan the training week with regard to the upcoming game.

Only when the points devised in the match plan are integrated into the training week through practical drills does all the work pay off.

Good results are often achieved with 11v11 drills because this is the most realistic form of play for implementing the points in the match plan.

Here the coach can constantly interrupt and simulate scenarios.

If there are not 22 players available, the squad could possibly be completed with youth players or players from the B team or by finding a test game opponent who is very similar to the upcoming opponent.

If this is not possible, the focus of training should be placed on group tactics. If using group tactics, it is important that the drills are always done in a tactically original space.

In addition to the playing field, video analysis and the coach board as well as individual and group discussions can be incorporated into training to embed the match plan in the players' minds.

The most important points are covered again just before the game and are posted in written form in the locker room because some players respond better to visuals.

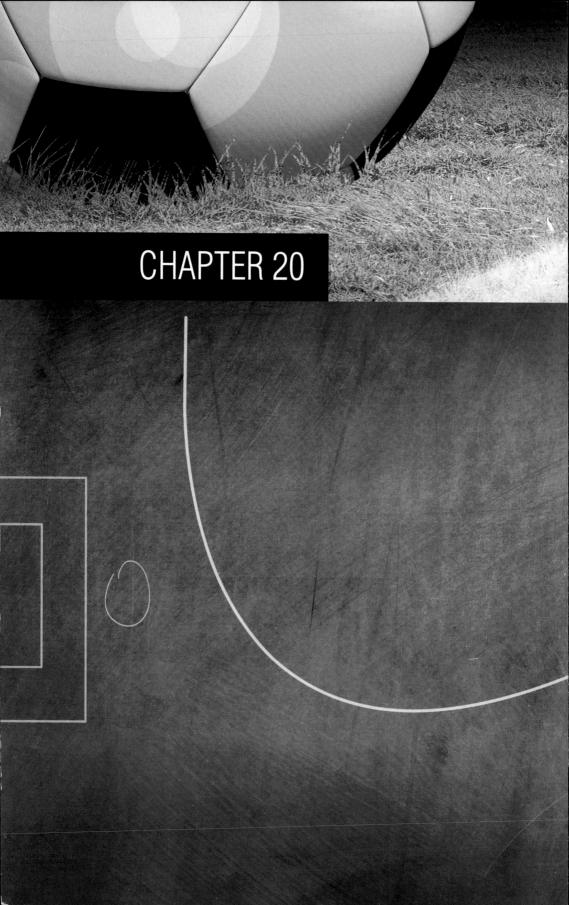

CHAPTER 20

Outlook

CHAPTER 20

Outlook

"Success is modern."

Finally, the question that arises is: How will soccer evolve?

It is a fact that soccer will continue to evolve. This is what the legendary coach Dettmar Cramer has to say on the subject in a great spot advertisement:

"Good isn't good enough as long as better is possible."

Dettmar Cramer at the coach board

As with everything else in life, soccer will evolve true to the motto "higher, faster, farther."

The following points will play an important role in the process.

- The renaissance of the center forward against extremely defensive teams.
- The difference in quality between top club teams and national teams will become greater.
- Anticipation and action speed will become more important because the playing field is becoming narrower.
- There will be more and more goals scored from set plays, such as standard situations.
- Open space and time will become increasingly scarce.
- The players' action speed will, therefore, continue to increase.
- Modern soccer players will have to be more and more flexible.
- Transitions between different systems will become more fluid.
- Successful teams can adjust to different game situations at all times and are equally proficient in different systems of play.
- Systems of play will tend to be more offensive.
- Some trends tend to repeat themselves. A good example is Greece's 2004 European Championship win with a sweeper.

Surprise: 2004 European Champion Greece wins with a sweeper.

- But the development steps will not be as significant as they were 40 or 50 years ago.
- Playing ability will become more and more relevant in soccer: How quickly can a player read new game situations and optimally manage them by using his tactical, technical, and athletic skills?
- The players will increasingly become "specialized all-rounders."
- Soccer will also evolve with regard to fitness. The players have to be faster and sprint more often.
- For this reason, the players' athletic training will need to become more soccer-specific and even position-specific. A wing player cannot possibly complete the same endurance training as a central defender.
- It is always good to take the occasional look at other sports like American football or hockey, which are ahead of soccer in terms of athletic- and position-specific training.
- Another trend is creative action on defense. Deliberate pressing strategies that control the opponent were hardly conceivable in the past.
- The future development of ball-oriented play will also be interesting: The first groups of players who received ball-oriented training at a very early age are now graduating from their youth teams.
- Another point of departure is the integration of specialty coaches, which has been standard procedure in many other sports.
- Many Swiss clubs have already begun to implement this by, for instance, hiring special coaches for strikers.
- Why should there not be a special coach for standard situations? After all, more than 20% of top-level goals are scored from standard situations.
- Head ball soccer will continue to become more relevant. Many youth organizations are already reacting to this reality, and the soccer pendulum is making a comeback.

- In addition, the training time will increase—not necessarily just on the field. For instance, using video analysis or maybe working on tactics and systems of play will become increasingly important parts of training.

- Facts, facts, facts! Modern computer systems make it possible to increasingly break down and analyze the game, which is why there is a need for more personnel to evaluate these details.

- Improved incorporation and interweaving between professional and youth organizations in which promising players are incorporated sooner and are also mentored longer during their first steps into the realm of professional soccer.

- Using facts through creativity: Examples would be a preplanned misdirected pass played behind the opposing defense to deliberately press them, because the possibility of scoring a goal from a press is relatively high. Another example would be to exploit the high error rate for throw-ins by deliberately throwing the ball across the sideline as close to the opponent's goal as possible to be able to press from there.

- 1v1 defense against the top players: Why should a Philipp Lahm not be able to neutralize a Lionel Messi with a direct 1v1 defense? The rest of the team plays 10v10 as usual.

- The coach's position and that of his coaching staff will become more important as they must devise measures to make sure the team can keep up with the trends.

In the words of Otto Rehhagel:

"In the end the truth can be found on the field!"

CREDITS

Cover design: Sabine Groten

Cover photo: ©imago-Sportfotodienst

Jacket design: Claudia Sakyi

Layout: Claudia Sakyi

Typesetting: www.satzstudio-hilger.de

Interior photos: ©iStock/Thinkstock
(Pg. 9 and chapter headers)

©picture-alliance/dpa
(Pg. 12, 14, 18, 24, 25, 26, 27, 28, 31, 34, 37, 46, 47, 48, 49, 51, 52, 53, 55, 56, 58, 64, 66, 70, 79, 81, 84, 85, 91, 94, 101, 104, 107, 109, 112, 133, 136, 142, 144, 166, 187, 190, 199, 201, 205, 209, 212, 229, 233, 236, 237)
©imago-Sportfotodienst
(Pg. 40, 43, 44, 59, 60, 89, 122, 128, 131, 198)

Graphics: easy Sports-Graphics
www.easy-sports-software.com

Copyediting: Elizabeth Evans

GERMAN SOCCER SECRETS

Tim Meyer/Oliver Faude/Karen aus der Fünten

SPORTS MEDICINE FOR FOOTBALL

Insight from Professional Football for All Levels of Play

This book provides the reader with advice on the treatment and prevention of illnesses and injuries in football. The most recent discoveries in performance diagnostics provide them with better tools to address the players' fitness requirements. The authors provide up-to-date sports medical findings and make them accessible for the readers.

All information subject to change © Thinkstock/iStock/Aksonov

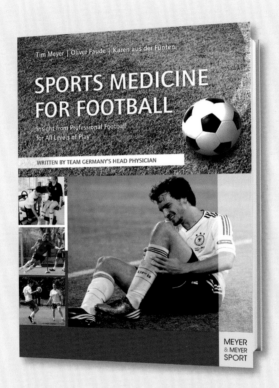

c. 200 p., in color, c. 150 photos + illus., paperback, 6 1/2" x 9 1/4"

ISBN: 9781782550471

$ 22.95 US/$ 45.95 AUS/£ 16.95 UK/€ 22.95

MEYER & MEYER
Fachverlag
Von-Coels-Str. 390
52080 Aachen
Germany

Phone   +49 02 41 - 9 58 10 - 13
Fax   +49 02 41 - 9 58 10 - 10
E-Mail   vertrieb@m-m-sports.com
Website   www.m-m-sports.com

All books available as E-books.

MEYER
& MEYER
SPORT

FURTHER BOOKS
ABOUT SOCCER

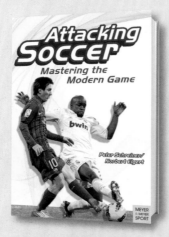

160 p., in color, 16 photos,

109 illus., paperback,

6 1/2" x 9 1/4"

ISBN: 9781782550082

$ 16.95 US/$ 29.95 AUS/

£ 12.95 UK/€ 16.95

Peter Schreiner/Norbert Elgert

ATTACKING
SOCCER
Mastering the Modern Game

Soccer fans around the world adore the style of play based on fast passing combinations and spectacular dribblings. The question is how to coach your team to embrace fast attacking soccer. With this book, every coach can shape his training programs with easy to use excersises.

Peter Schreiner

SOCCER – PERFECT BALL CONTROL

Want to learn how to dribble and feint like Maradona or Ronaldinho, and to juggle the ball like Jay-Jay Okocha or Edgar Davids? In this book, players learn how to become good ball handlers and master tricks that enable them to score more goals while playing attractive, offensive soccer.

2nd edition

208 p., in color, 212 photos,
130 illus., paperback,
6 1/2" x 9 1/4"

ISBN: 9781841262789

$ 17.95 US/$ 29.95 AUS/
£ 12.95 UK/€ 16.95

MEYER & MEYER
Fachverlag
Von-Coels-Str. 390
52080 Aachen
Germany

Phone   +49 02 41 - 9 58 10 - 13
Fax   +49 02 41 - 9 58 10 - 10
E-Mail vertrieb@m-m-sports.com
Website www.m-m-sports.com

All books available as E-books.

MEYER
& MEYER
SPORT